Exploring the Bible
THE DICKINSON SERIES

INTRODUCING THE NEW TESTAMENT

Leader's Guide Large Print Edition
Second Edition

Rev. Anne Robertson

Foreword by Exploring the Bible benefactor,
Dr. Charles C. Dickinson III

MASSACHUSETTS BIBLE SOCIETY
One Book, Many Voices

Copyright © June 2013 by the Massachusetts Bible Society
Copyright © 2nd Edition 2015

All rights reserved. No part of this book may be reproduced, stored in a retrieval system, or transmitted in any form or by any means, electronic, mechanical, including photocopying, recording, or otherwise, without the written permission of the publisher.

Unless otherwise indicated, Bible quotations in this book are from the New Revised Standard Version Bible, copyright © 1989 by the National Council of Churches of Christ in the U.S.A. Used by permission. All rights reserved.

Massachusetts Bible Society
199 Herrick Road
Newton Centre, MA 02459

Book design by Thomas Bergeron
www.thomasbergeron.com
Typeface: Jenson Pro, Gill Sans

ISBN-13: 978-0-9907212-8-4

2ND EDITION

*For my mother
Joan Ruth Robertson Thompson
May 26, 1932–October 18, 2012*

*Your hymns rocked me to sleep.
Your love and faith formed my own.
Your life showed me Christ.
I sing now for you.
With you.
One.*

"The glory that you have given me I have given them, so that they may be one, as we are one, I in them and you in me, that they may become completely one, so that the world may know that you have sent me and have loved them even as you have loved me."

John 17:22–23

TABLE OF CONTENTS

Acknowledgments

Welcome
Introducing <u>Exploring the Bible: The Dickinson Series</u>	iii
Our Theological Point of View	viii
Course Administration	viii

Leading Exploring the Bible: The Dickinson Series
Your Students	xi
Your Class	xix
You Are a Facilitator	xxii
Becoming a Registered Group Leader	xxvii

Overview of Class Session Elements
Check-In	xxix
Bible Activity	xxx
Life Connection Activity	xxxi
Review of Homework	xxxi
Extra Mile Presentations	xxxii
First and Last Sessions	xxxiii

Lesson Plans
Session 1: Son of Man	1
Session 2: Son of David	11
Session 3: Son of God	17
Session 4: Man of Letters	25
Session 5: Leadership	35
Session 6: Experiencing Church	43

Forms, Handouts, and Supplemental Material
Form: Student Evaluation	53
Form: Facilitator Evaluation	59
Massachusetts Bible Society Statement on Scripture	63
A Covenant for Bible Study	64
Session 1 Handout: Class Contact Information	65
Session 1 Handout: LIfe in Nazareth Quiz	67
Session 3 Handout: I Am	69

TABLE OF CONTENTS

Forms, Handouts, and Supplemental Material (Cont.)

Session 4 Handout: Connect the Dots Worksheet	77
Session 4 Handout: Connect the Dots City List	79
Session 4 Handout: Asia Minor Map Solution	81
Sample Advertising Blurbs for <u>Introducing the New Testament</u>	83
Glossary from Student Text	84

Acknowledgments

This course is the last in the three-course series Exploring the Bible: The Dickinson Series. As with the previous courses, I have to first acknowledge Dr. Charles Dickinson, whose gifts of time, expertise, and treasure have made this entire series possible. You can read more about him on p. v and can watch a brief video about his hopes for this series on the exploringthebible.org website.

Special thanks go to Rev. John Stendahl, our Board President and Pastor of the Lutheran Church of the Newtons in Newton Centre, MA. John has a special heart for interfaith work and, with his keen theological mind, was able to help me shape the material in Appendix 4 of the Student Text, "Who Killed Jesus?" I am indebted to him for (I hope!) keeping me out of hot water in that section.

To be sure the material presented here is in keeping with the best scholarship, Dr. Wayne Meeks, Woolsey Professor Emeritus of Religious Studies at Yale, was kind enough to review the material for accuracy. I am grateful for his corrections, suggestions, and overall support.

I also continue to be indebted to the following congregations and group leaders who have served as pilot groups to test the effectiveness of both the Student Text and the class sessions outlined in the Leader's Guide: Dr. Ellen Porter Honnet and Jacqui James at the First Unitarian Society of Newton (West Newton, MA); Lynne Osborn at St. Matthew's United Methodist Church (Acton, MA); Aurelio Ramirez at the Lutheran Church of the Newtons (Newton, MA); Frances Taylor, Director of Faith Formation at Sacred Heart Parish (Lynn, MA); and Rev. Dr. Thomas D. Wintle at First Parish Church (Weston, MA). They had to deal with this material in its raw, unedited form, and their feedback has been critical to shaping this final product.

Our production team continues their awesome work, from editor Nancy Fitzgerald, copyeditor Jennifer Hackett, proofreader Maria Boyer, and designer Thomas Bergeron, to the amazing staff I am privileged to work with at the Massachusetts Bible Society: Jocelyn Bergeron, Michael Colyott, and Frank Stevens. The MBS Trustees and retired editing professional Ms. Cynthia Thompson are also to be commended for their work in offering feedback on the materials and reaching out to find appropriate places to offer and endorse these courses.

In Gratitude,

Anne Robertson

Welcome

Introducing Exploring the Bible: The Dickinson Series

<u>Exploring the Bible: The Dickinson Series</u> is a series of three, six-week courses that leads to a Certificate in Biblical Literacy from the historic Massachusetts Bible Society.

Each of the three courses is designed to fit six ninety-minute sessions with a group of eight to fifteen people. The Massachusetts Bible Society provides training, materials, and ongoing support for those who would like to run the program in their local churches or communities. Those leading the courses are not expected to be biblical experts or pastors. They are those gifted and trained to facilitate a warm, welcoming, and open group environment where the material can be presented and discussed with respect for all participants.

The Exploring the Bible Program

Three Courses: A Bird's-Eye View

I. **What Is the Bible?** A broad overview of the Bible, including chapters on how to select a Bible suitable for your needs, how the Bible is organized, how the collection of books that comprise the Bible were chosen, different ways that people approach the text, and what archaeology has to tell us about the text and its stories.

II. Introducing the Old Testament. A look at the best-known stories, most influential passages, and unforgettable characters that comprise the Old Testament. What are the primary themes and narratives? What are the characteristics of ancient Hebrew literature and the mindset of people in the ancient Near East? Explore both the writings themselves and the historical contexts that gave them birth.

III. Introducing the New Testament. Learn about Jesus as a man, as a Jewish rabbi, and as the Christ of Christian faith. Explore first-century Nazareth, what ancient letter-writing practices can tell us about Paul's letters, and the wild apocalypse of Revelation.

Online Resources

Join us for discussion on the Exploring the Bible Facebook page and follow us on Twitter @ExploreBible and swap questions and experiences with others across the country and across the world who are doing the courses in their local communities. Many of you are asking for the opportunity to take the courses online and we hope to be able to offer that down the road. And you can always check out our website at exploringthebible.org for other news, recommended reading, and to find a course near you.

The Exploring the Bible Students

The series is designed for two distinct types of students:

The Casual or Informal Students. The first group is made up of those who might know something about the Bible but have gaps in their knowledge, or those who just want to test the waters of biblical studies. These students might want simply to take one of the three courses or put together some combination of those components without doing all that is necessary to complete the certificate program. While it's expected that this second group will still actively participate in whatever course(s) they select, there is less work expected of them outside the group setting.

The Intentional or "Extra Mile" Students. The second group represents those who have determined that they really want to do some work to build a strong foundation for Bible study. They might be Christians considering seminary, people of faith who don't know their own Scriptures very well, people of other faiths who want a clearer understanding of the Christian text, or even people of no faith who recognize the cultural and geopolitical influence of the Bible and want to understand it better. The common denominator among this group is that they want to do the whole program, including the "Extra Mile" assignments required to earn the Certificate of Biblical Literacy or Continuing Education Units (CEUs).

We hope each study group will consist of both casual and more intentional learners, and our design includes opportunities in class sessions for those engaging the material more deeply to share what they've learned with the others.

The Exploring the Bible Sponsors

The Benefactor

Exploring the Bible: The Dickinson Series is named in honor of its chief benefactor, Dr. Charles C. Dickinson III, a biblical scholar and long-time trustee of the Massachusetts Bible Society. Dr. Charles Dickinson was born in Charleston, West Virginia, on May 13, 1936; was educated there and at Phillips Academy, Andover, Massachusetts; and graduated cum laude in religion and philosophy from Dartmouth College, Hanover, New Hampshire. After serving three and a half years with the US Marine Corps in the USA and Far East, he studied theology and philosophy in Chicago, Pittsburgh, West and East Germany, at Yale University, and at Union Theological Seminary in New York. He received his B.D. (Bachelor of Divinity) and Ph.D. degrees in Pittsburgh in 1965 and 1973 respectively and did post-doctoral study at Oxford University and Harvard Divinity School. Dr. Dickinson has taught in Richmond, Virginia; Kinshasa, Zaire, Congo; Charleston, West Virginia; Rome, Italy; the People's Republic of China; Andover Newton Theological School; and Beacon Hill Seminars in Boston. He lives with his wife, JoAnne, and their son, John, in Boston.

The Author

This series was conceived and designed by Rev. Anne Robertson, executive director of the Massachusetts Bible Society, who also developed and wrote the three student texts and leader's guides. She is the author of three additional books: <u>Blowing the Lid Off the God-Box: Opening Up to a Limitless Faith</u> (Morehouse, 2005); <u>God's Top 10: Blowing the Lid Off the Commandments</u> (Morehouse, 2006); and <u>God with Skin On: Finding God's Love in Human Relationships</u> (Morehouse, 2009). Rev. Robertson is an elder in the New England Conference of the United Methodist Church, is a winner of the Wilbur C. Ziegler Award for Excellence in Preaching, and is a sought-after speaker and workshop leader. She can be found on the web at www.annerobertson.org.

The Massachusetts Bible Society

Founded on July 6, 1809, the Massachusetts Bible Society is an ecumenical, Christian organization that has historically been a place where those across the theological spectrum of belief could unite for a common purpose. At the beginning of its history, that purpose was simply getting a copy of the Bible into the hands of anyone who wanted one, especially those without the means or opportunity to obtain one themselves. In more recent times, that work has been supplemented by the development of a variety of educational programs highlighting the importance of the Bible for faith, culture, history, and politics, as well as providing a forum for the many different voices of biblical interpretation. Exploring the Bible is a significant addition to those efforts and attempts to continue the historic tradition of being a place where those of many different faith traditions can unite for a common purpose—in this case, biblical literacy. You can find out more about the Massachusetts Bible Society at www.massbible.org.

You

Exploring the Bible: The Dickinson Series is made possible because you have elected to be a part of it. While we believe the course materials are useful in and of themselves, it is the community of students and group leaders who bring those materials to life as you engage with one another in your classes and online forums. Just by participating, you are helping to raise the level of biblical literacy in our world. You can ensure that this ministry continues by completing the facilitator and student evaluations for each course, by purchasing the materials, and by telling others about Exploring the Bible: The Dickinson Series. There are also opportunities for you to provide scholarship assistance for future students, to attend training to become a group leader, or simply to offer moral or financial support to the mission of the Massachusetts Bible Society. Our most important sponsor is you. Find out how you can help at exploringthebible.org.

Our Theological Point of View

In the creation of this series there are several obvious biases:

- The Bible is a book that can and should be read by individuals both inside and outside the church.
- Understanding of the Bible is enhanced and deepened in conversation with others.
- The tools of scholarship are not incompatible with a faithful reading of Scripture.
- Diversity of opinion is both a welcome and a necessary part of any education—especially biblical education.

Beyond those points we have tried to give an unbiased theological perspective, describing differences of opinion and scholarship in neutral terms. Although named for and written by Christians, Exploring the Bible: The Dickinson Series is designed to be an educational tool, not an evangelistic tool. The Massachusetts Bible Society affirms that the making of Christian disciples is the job of the local church. These materials are designed either to fit into the overall disciple-making effort of a local church or into a secular environment where people of other faiths or of no faith can gain a deeper understanding of the nature and content of the Bible.

Course Administration

Obtaining Credit for Certification or CEUs

Those wishing to enroll in the certificate program or obtain CEUs for their work must fill out an application and do the work in an approved small-group setting. Those who simply work their way through the materials on their own are not eligible for credit or certification.

You can find out all the details and download any necessary forms at exploringthebible.org/getting-credit.

Note that you must be a registered group leader with the Massachusetts Bible Society for any of your students to get credit. This is not difficult to obtain and is not necessary for leading an informal group. But you must register for any of your students to receive formal credit. You can find the application at exploringthebible.org/forms.

The Cost

Costs will vary depending on whether you are a casual student (which has no cost apart from the books) or are taking the course either for CEUs or certification (for which there is a fee). Please check our website at exploringthebible.org/getting-credit for more information, current rates, and information on discounts and scholarships.

Keeping in Touch

Go to exploringthebible.org to learn more or contact the Massachusetts Bible Society at 199 Herrick Road, Newton Centre, MA 02459 or dsadmin@massbible.org. You may also call us at 617-969-9404.

Note About Page References

The notation "LP" after a page number indicates the large print version of the Student Text.

Leading Exploring the Bible: The Dickinson Series

(Note: Some people contact the Massachusetts Bible Society in search of someone who would lead a group in their location. If you would be interested in such an opportunity, please contact us.)

Your Students

The Exploring the Bible student materials can be used by anyone, whether they're part of a formal class or not. It's designed, however, for a group of eight to fifteen adults to study together, and students will gain the most from the series if they participate in such a group. You may be part of a church or other organization that has recruited you to facilitate the class, or you may have just picked up the materials on your own and decided that you wanted to lead a group in your community. Either way, there are things to think about when putting a group together.

Who Would Be Interested in This Course?

There are three groups of people whose interest might be piqued by this series:

First are those for whom it is primarily designed: People who know little to nothing about the Bible and its contents. They don't know Adam from Abraham from Jesus and couldn't name a Bible story if you paid them. They might be Christians seeking knowledge of their own sacred text, members of another religion who want to learn about the Bible, or those of no particular faith at all who simply recognize the cultural, historical, and social impact of the Bible on world civilization. What they have in common is that, for all intents and purposes, they have never cracked open a Bible. Especially if they are Christians in a church, this group may be embarrassed to admit their degree of biblical illiteracy.

Second, there are many, many people who know a good bit about the contents of the Bible but next to nothing about the context of the Bible—for example, how it was put together and when, the history and culture of biblical times, and so on. This second group may also find a great benefit in <u>Exploring the Bible: The Dickinson Series</u> because of the inclusion of that type of information in the materials and exercises.

Third, there are (for want of a better term) Bible study "junkies." Found mostly (although not exclusively) in churches, these folks will sign up for anything at all with the Bible in the title on the off chance that there may still be some teensy bit of biblical information they're lacking.

Each of these groups can find some benefit in the study—no matter how much you already know about the Bible there is always more to learn, especially as you discuss passages with others. Problems may arise, however, when the various knowledge levels are grouped together, because the questions and issues that come up are qualitatively different for each type of group.

For example, groups two and three might start comparing this Bible text to another while group one is still trying to figure out who the characters in the story are. As the discussions move on without them, referencing stories and texts with which the first group is entirely unfamiliar, the first group starts to feel dumb and drops out, and you lose the very type of student the course is designed to help.

With some finesse and discussion control by the facilitator, the first two types of students can be mixed in the same class without too many difficulties (although ideally there would be one group of pure neophytes and a second group of those lacking only the contextual piece). The third group, however, really needs to be actively discouraged from taking the class as a student, unless the whole class has substantial knowledge. Otherwise they will almost certainly hinder learning in others.

I have seen this time and time again in groups designed for beginning Bible students. The junkies come, monopolize the discussions, and soon the real neophytes are dropping out with an apologetic, "Oh, I thought this was just for new people." Your Bible junkies should be encouraged to facilitate a class themselves or, if there are enough of them, a class could be made up of just this type of student. They also could be encouraged to simply read the materials on their own.

If the person absolutely cannot be dissuaded from attending (or if to do so will cause too much conflict), consider giving them some sort of title or special advisory role in the group—perhaps as a co-facilitator. This will at least keep other students from feeling embarrassed about their knowledge by comparison.

Getting the Right People Together

The key to having groups that are basically on the same level of Bible knowledge is both in your initial advertising and in your follow-up with those who express an interest. At the end of this guide on page 83 are some advertising blurbs you can use to announce the course and solicit interest. You can also, of course, write your own. To avoid the pitfalls of mixing incompatible Bible knowledge levels, it will be most helpful if your advertising asks people to contact you (or whoever is receiving the information) in order to "express interest" rather than "sign up." That gives you the opportunity for a follow-up conversation in which you can find out the person's relative level of biblical knowledge and make appropriate recommendations.

In gauging the level, don't give an impromptu Bible pop-quiz; just ask something along these lines: "We like to put together groups of people with similar levels of knowledge about the Bible. A lot of people—even in churches—really don't know the Bible at all, others know a number of the stories but don't really know how the Bible itself was put together or they may struggle in reading it. Still others have taken lots of Bible studies and are eager to know even more. Do you see yourself in any of those groups? Why are you interested in this course?"

A conversation like that allows you to let people know the parameters of whatever group is set up without sounding like you are giving anyone preferential treatment. Some possible responses to your callers' comments: "Gosh, Sarah, the only people who responded are those who don't even have a basic knowledge of the Sunday School stories. We have enough for that group but we didn't get enough for a group at your level of knowledge. We might even have enough for two of those basic groups. Would you possibly be interested in leading one?" Or, "Well, Zach, we have enough for a group, but most of them have a lot more experience with the Bible than you do. You're more than welcome to come to the class if you're comfortable with that—after all, the material was designed for those who haven't even cracked the book—or you can wait for another group. It's your call."

Ideally you should establish the dates and times for the class and begin advertising for students two to three months before the time of the first class, maybe more if you're part of a busy organization that schedules events six months to a year out. Give people enough time to get the dates on their calendars so that you can ensure the best attendance possible.

Advertise the course in places where the students you want to attract will see it. If you represent a church that wants to reach out into the community with this course, advertising only in the church bulletin or on the church website will not help you achieve your goal. And don't forget to mention the class on social media. If you are open to people outside of your church or community attending your class, go to exploringthebible.org to list your class for those who might be looking for a venue near them.

Opening Up to the Community

The Massachusetts Bible Society often hears from people who are looking for a Bible study course in their area. Because Exploring the Bible offers Continuing Education Units (CEUs) and a certificate program (for those who do the Extra Mile work in the Student Text), we would like to know if you'd be willing to accept student referrals from the Massachusetts Bible Society for your group.

If so, we'll be glad to post the details of your class on our website to let interested parties know where they can find a course and we will advertise your course to our e-mail list. To make this manageable for you, please be sure to set a registration deadline and send the information to us as soon as you know it.

We also receive occasional requests from churches or other organizations that would like to run a course but don't have a leader. If you would be willing to facilitate the course for others, please drop us a line and let us know.

Students Who Miss a Class

Class dates, times, and locations should be established far enough in advance that students can plan their schedules in a way that minimizes conflicts with other activities. From your initial contact with potential students onward, the importance of attending class, both for themselves and for others in the class, should be stressed.

Even so, scheduling conflicts will come up and students will miss classes from time to time. Those seeking CEUs or the full Certificate in Biblical Literacy may miss one class, if necessary. The homework from the missed session, however, still must be completed. Those informal students who would like a completion certificate for this one course may miss up to two classes.

If students are missing more than two sessions, they are missing at least half the course and it's worth asking them whether they would like to simply wait and take it at a time that's better for them. Every person who attends enhances the learning of others in the class. Those who miss classes are not just missing an opportunity for their own education but are hampering the ability of others to have the full group experience.

If a student wants to make up a class, that is solely up to you as the group leader. If you want to take the extra time, that's your call. It is not necessary.

It is helpful for you to have a backup leader, however, in case you have to miss a class for any reason.

Students Who Don't Do Homework

Your initial contact with potential students should include the information that there will be homework in the course—to a greater or lesser degree, depending on the level of recognition they are seeking. **The homework for informal students ranges from about twenty minutes to two and a half hours per week, depending on the session and the course. Extra Mile students can count on several hours each week.**

As with class attendance, the expectations are greater for those seeking CEUs or certification. Continuing Education Units and progress toward the full Certificate in Biblical Literacy will only be granted when all the regular and Extra Mile homework has been completed and not more than one class session has been missed. Completion certificates for informal students will only be granted when the facilitator verifies that the student has come to class prepared and has not missed more than two sessions.

You will, most likely, have at least a couple of students who simply don't complete the reading assignments, week after week. Sessions are designed so that even these students should be able to get something out of the class session. Be sure your students realize that it's better to come to class unprepared than not to come at all. They can still learn—they just won't have as rich an experience as they would otherwise.

If you notice that very few are able to complete the reading, you might consider holding sessions less frequently—perhaps every other week instead of every week, for example. Courses two and three have considerably more reading than course one, and if you have participants with busy lives they might appreciate a longer time frame. Of course if they are still just going to wait until the night before to try to cram it all in, having a longer stretch will not help.

Some reminders are built into the curriculum. The last element of every class session is a review of the homework for the coming week. You might also want to send an e-mail midweek to jog your students' memory—perhaps with a teaser from one of the questions for reflection in the Student Text. If someone has posted on the Exploring the Bible Facebook page, you could also send a brief e-mail notice inviting students to check out the new thread or new response.

Don't make a spectacle of or chide students who frequently are not prepared, especially in front of others. It's often helpful, however, to have a private conversation with such a student to see what the issues are that are preventing the work from being done. You might be able to offer some solutions or guidance. Remember the great caveat of Plato: "Be kind, for everyone is fighting a great battle." When your students finally meet God face to face, nobody is going to be asking them why they didn't do their Exploring the Bible homework. Keep perspective.

Dealing With Problem Personalities

One of the most difficult parts of leading any group, no matter what the topic, is the truly problem personality. While everyone can have a bad day and some people have quirks that can cause awkward moments, sometimes you'll run across participants who prevent the group from accomplishing its goals. They might consistently dominate the discussion and pull the group off track, make comments that are offensive and/or threatening, or exhibit other behaviors that either destroy the open and inclusive atmosphere or make getting through the material impossible.

If you should end up with "that guy" or "that gal" in your group and repeated attempts at (private) correction have not yielded a change in behavior, please talk either with your pastor or the Massachusetts Bible Society to resolve the issue. In rare cases a person might have to be asked to leave the group. And whatever you do, make sure you don't become "that guy" or "that gal"!

Your Class

Group Size

The session activities in this Leader's Guide assume a group size of eight to fifteen people. Sessions often call for the students to be divided into smaller groups for discussion. This both saves time and allows those who are reticent to speak up in a larger group to still have input and express their views.

This course will be challenging to do with fewer than eight students. Over the course of the study, someone will get sick, someone will suddenly be without transportation, someone's child will have a recital, someone will get called in to work, and you will find yourself trying to do a session with two students. Without a rich and varied discussion in class, students are not receiving the full benefit of the course, even if they are one of the two students who did show up. If you cannot recruit a class of at least eight students, consider rescheduling the course for another time or make sure you really have an attendance commitment from the ones you have.

If your church is small, consider reaching out to other churches in your area. These courses have been used successfully with both ecumenical and interfaith groups as well as groups that include atheists and agnostics. Think beyond the walls of your church or organization.

This course will be difficult to do with more than fifteen students. And fifteen is pushing it. This is a small-group study. With more than fifteen students it is easy to lose the intimacy that allows for the trust, bonding, and sharing that make small groups such a powerful learning environment. You will also be hard-pressed to keep within the session time frame of ninety minutes. If you have more than fifteen who are interested, consider dividing them into two classes.

If you have a large group and five or more are Extra Mile students (see p. v), you might also consider having one class of only those more intentional learners. Since they cannot receive the certificate or CEUs without full completion of the course (see p. viii), you are less likely to have attendance issues in that group.

As you progress beyond Course One in the series, you may have new students who have not taken the previous courses. This is especially true of the New Testament course, since many Christians tend to think the Old Testament is irrelevant and might skip the first courses to wait for the "real Bible." Our evaluations have shown that sometimes this has been a hurdle for the new students. The early courses give some important background both on the Bible itself and on the overall purpose and approach of the course. And, of course, a solid understanding of the Old Testament is critical for a proper understanding of the New.

While there is no need to forbid students to jump in to a later course if they haven't done the early ones, you should let them know that others who have done so have not gotten the same benefit as those who took the courses in order. You could also encourage such students to get the student books for the other courses to read in preparation.

Meeting Location

Your meeting space can either help or hinder the students' learning and will send unconscious messages about how open people should be about their thoughts and circumstances. While this is a class for which some students will receive various kinds of credit, a classroom atmosphere of students lined up in rows (or pews) in front of a teacher will not be ideal. Students should be in a setting where they can easily see one another as well as the facilitator, can engage in discussions (either in one group or in sub-groups), can enjoy refreshments without worry, and can sit for an hour and a half without discomfort.

Be sure to look for a space that can accommodate students with mobility issues or other types of disabilities. Remember that each course's Student Text is available in both regular and large print.

If you're leading a group in which everyone is familiar with one another and you're not accepting any referral students, then meeting in someone's home is ideal. If you're a church group, meeting in a home means you don't have to worry that six other groups want the church lounge the same night you want it, and the home atmosphere can make people feel…well…at home. Do be sure, however, that it is a home that, at least for that time, will be relatively free of distractions and that it can comfortably accommodate the number of people in your group.

If you want to draw in some new folks to your group, it's better to find a public location. This might be the aforementioned church lounge, a library or community center with available meeting space, or your local pub or coffee shop. As the group gets to know one another, you might decide to move elsewhere, but at the outset meet at a location that group members can easily find and get to.

Don't discount the possibility of hosting the class at another institution. Want students from the nearby college? Call the chaplain and see about getting space for the class on campus. Want to help seniors at the local assisted-living facility keep their minds active? See if you can use space right there. Does your congregation have an active prison outreach? Teach it there. A good host is always planning for the ease and comfort of the guests. Model biblical hospitality in your meeting space.

You Are a Facilitator

Many people feel intimidated by the thought of leading a Bible study. There is the perception that to lead people through a study of the Bible, one must be a learned biblical scholar or a pastor. That would be true if the course leader were developing the materials to be taught. With Exploring the Bible, however, the Massachusetts Bible Society has provided material that is grounded in solid biblical scholarship but that can be presented by those without specific biblical training. As a group leader, you are a facilitator, not a teacher. The information is in the books, you are just there to help people find their way through it.

Of course there's nothing wrong with having a biblical scholar or pastor lead this course. It is simply our belief that such qualification is not necessary to effectively introduce students to the Bible. You can do this!

But I Don't Know the Answers!

Undoubtedly there will be class sessions in which questions arise that aren't addressed in the Student Text or Leader's Guide. When that happens and you don't know the answer, don't panic. You're not in this alone. Let's review your options for dealing with questions that stump you. Whatever option you choose, please be sure to record the question.

If the same question keeps popping up in different groups, we'll know we should address it in a revision of the Student Text.

- If the question is specific to a particular Bible passage, ask students to look in the notes associated with that passage in their study Bibles. Ask: "Does anyone have notes that address the question?" This approach helps students familiarize themselves with how a study Bible can help them.

- If your meeting location has wi-fi access or a tech-savvy student has a smart phone, type the question into Google and see what comes up. This can help students see how to research their own questions when they arise outside a class setting. There are new Bible study tools appearing online all the time. You can find a listing of some we find helpful at www.massbible.org/how-to-study-bible.

- Suggest that someone submit the question to the Ask-a-Prof service of the Massachusetts Bible Society. This is a free service and can be found at www.massbible.org/ask-a-prof.

- Encourage students to "like" the Exploring the Bible Facebook page to discuss their questions with students in other groups and the Massachusetts Bible Society staff.

- Volunteer to research the question yourself and bring back a response the next week. In doing that research, you can ask other members of your church, check the Internet or library, or contact the Massachusetts Bible Society for a response.

- Remind students that not all questions have "answers" per se. Sometimes a variety of opinions will be the best you can do. Be sure students know that Appendix 8 on page 265 (p. 327 LP) in their Student Text suggests resources for finding answers to their questions.

Atmosphere Is Everything

Learning is more than absorbing a set of facts. To truly learn and grow, students must feel that their honest questions are taken seriously and that they won't be judged for expressing their opinions. Perhaps the most important role of the group leader is ensuring that the class environment is "safe" in that regard. Students are willing to take risks in learning when they feel a class environment is safe.

This course was not created as a tool for Christian evangelism and faith formation, although the Massachusetts Bible Society is certainly not opposed to such activities. With Exploring the Bible, however, we wanted to create a vehicle in which people of all faiths or no faith could learn more about the Bible for any and all reasons. We believe that faith formation is the role of the local church. What we have provided in Exploring the Bible is an educational tool that can be used to anchor that faith formation in local churches and to provide information about the Bible that can be accepted in secular and interfaith settings.

To make that possible, the class setting and atmosphere must work to embrace not only very, very basic questions (for example, "Is 'Christ' Jesus' last name?") with respect, but must also be open to those who might challenge traditional Christian interpretations or express dislike for biblical passages. Even if you have an entire group of professing Christians, there are probably beliefs and opinions in the room that contradict Christian orthodoxy or run afoul of the doctrines of a particular tradition or denomination. As long as the question is sincere and isn't coming from a problem personality purposely trying to stir the pot, your job is to make sure that the person asking feels heard and respected and that the question is given a fair hearing.

How the first such question is handled will determine the extent of real learning that can occur. Being able to hear challenging questions and comments without bristling is a much more important qualification for being a leader of these courses than Bible knowledge. Of course any statements that demean another race, gender, sexual orientation, or anything else should be swiftly corrected and apologized for.

Should the Leader Participate?

In most cases, the person leading the class should not participate as a class member in the exercises, even if you are learning the material along with the students. Any one of the exercises during class sessions could easily take up the entire class time. You're needed as a timekeeper and cannot fulfill that role as effectively if you're involved in discussion yourself. You should, however, be completely familiar with the exercise that the class is doing and with the material on which it's based. A thorough checklist for class preparation is provided at the beginning of each session's lesson plan.

You're also in a role of authority, even if you don't feel particularly authoritative. For some students, when the leader weighs in on a subject (especially when that leader is also a pastor or other respected person in the community), it can come across as pressure to conform to that leader's opinion. When that occurs, learning is stunted, since it may be perceived that not all opinions or positions can be freely considered.

That's not to say you must always remain silent and aloof. There may be an occasion when you need to participate for reasons of group cohesion. If, for example, a class has a member with a difficult personality who is making discussion in smaller groups difficult, you might volunteer to be that person's partner for one of the exercises. You should also step in to help de-escalate any conflicts, to protect those expressing unpopular opinions, to prod a stalled discussion, or to get a discussion back on track.

If group members are asking for your opinion, try to dissuade them or at least give your opinion last so that others don't feel constrained from expressing different thoughts. And even then, tread with caution. The authority figure speaking last can seem to negate or even mock all different responses that have been given prior. If you must weigh in, do so last and with a huge dose of humility and respect for other opinions expressed. When you can affirm any part of what someone else thinks, do so.

The only time more intentional participation might be warranted is if you end up with a group that is thinking rigidly and as a monolith. If there are no divergent opinions in the group, something is amiss either in class atmosphere or in student imagination. There are always differences of opinion among human beings, even if the people are part of the same faith tradition or even the same church.

If those alternative opinions are not being expressed, it's part of your job to break down whatever walls are keeping them out. That might involve you throwing out some different ideas for discussion, even if they're not opinions that you favor. Just keep your disfavor to yourself and encourage a discussion of the ideas on their own merits. That will help students to see that the expression of different opinions is not only safe but also encouraged and will help them learn to think outside the box.

Please Give Us Feedback

Near the back of this guide are course evaluations for both students and group leaders. Every Student Text has that same course evaluation in it and you can find it online at exploringthebible.org/forms. It is so helpful to us to receive these evaluations. The lesson plan for Session 6 includes time for evaluation and provides instructions for returning evaluations to us. Because these courses are being published in a print-on-demand format, we can make adjustments to the text very easily.

Whether you are letting us know about a typo that we missed or letting us know the ways that the course did or didn't work for you and your group, your feedback helps us to make this material the best it can be. We read every single evaluation that comes to us and while we love to hear praise and sometimes use those statements for testimonials, we truly want to know if something about the course material or presentation has been problematic. If the same criticisms keep coming across the desk, we fix the problem.

Please let us hear from you. It really helps.

Becoming a Registered Group Leader

If you just have informal students in your group, then there is no need to register with the Massachusetts Bible Society. If you have Extra Mile students who are seeking credit, however, they can only get that credit with a registered group leader. It isn't hard to register, but it is necessary for anyone in your group to get formal credit for their work.

To register, go to exploringthebible.org/forms and you will find two documents. One is the actual Application to Lead Groups for Credit and the other is the document that spells out the details of working with students seeking credit. The latter document is under "Other Documents of Interest" on the Forms page and is called "Expectations and Requirements for Leading a Group for Credit." Read that and send us the application.

If you have any questions, feel free to call or e-mail us.

Overview of Class Session Elements

Check-In

Beginning in Session 2, each class session begins with a set of two check-in questions about the material to be dealt with in that session:

- What is one thing I have learned from this material?
- What is one question I have related to this week's topic?

These questions are posed in the Student Text to help participants prepare for the next class, so ideally they have already thought about them. **These are not designed to be discussion questions. Responses should be one or two sentences at most, simply stated by students without any elaboration.** It's simply a way to gauge where students are and to allow participants to hear, in their classmates' responses, questions or issues they may not have thought about themselves. It is also a helpful tool to get people focused on the material at hand and to remember some of the themes and stories they read about.

One way to assure that check-in time doesn't turn into a full-blown discussion is to simply record the responses on your white board or newsprint or on paper. That way, questions won't get lost in the shuffle and if there isn't a sufficient response during the rest of the class session it can be carried over or addressed through one of the means discussed in the "But I Don't Know the Answers" section on page xxii. **This technique of writing questions to be answered later is often called the "Parking Lot"—a place to park your questions and issues for a bit to see if they're answered by later activity.**

Bible Activity

Most sessions contain a thirty-minute activity that examines a particular biblical passage or story in detail. The goal of this activity is to become more familiar with a well-known Bible story or passage and to get some practice thinking critically about the text. Students will be divided into two or more groups and encouraged to use the resources in their study Bibles as well as the text itself.

For some students, this program will represent an entirely new way of looking at the Bible and could be unsettling at times, depending on their background. Go gently in such instances and respect the struggles some might have in, for example, finding that the creation stories in Genesis 1 and Genesis 2–3 don't match. Don't rush to find solutions, but don't dismiss student concerns, either. You may want to ask some students to formulate their concerns into questions or issues that can be put in the Parking Lot to see if further light is shed along the way.

The Bible Activity is usually wrapped up with groups reporting back in some way about what they've discovered in their study of the text.

Life Connection Activity

Most sessions also contain a thirty-minute activity on a second well-known passage of the Bible. The difference is that in this activity the questions are more reflective. Here the objective is to explore the ways in which the Bible has relevance in daily life—either in the individual life of the student or in the broader scope of community and culture.

When students are asked to reflect more personally about a Bible passage, the groups are typically smaller (two to three people) so that it's a bit easier to open up to someone else. These responses are typically not conveyed to the group at large but are left in the sharing of the small groups.

In both the Bible and Life Connection Activities, students will learn more if they're with different groups each week. Encourage students to group with those they haven't before and recommend that couples and close friends split up into different pairs or groupings for these exercises. If there is great reluctance to do this, it need not be forced, but do keep trying for new group permutations.

Review of Homework

The Student Text contains homework—one assignment for all students and a second assignment for those seeking certification or CEUs. The latter are referred to as the Extra Mile students, and in order to earn their certification, they must complete **both** sets of homework. At the end of each session, spend about five minutes looking over the homework for the next session to resolve any questions and to offer a constant reminder that there is homework to be done.

Extra Mile Presentations

To be sure that those who have chosen to engage in more in-depth study of the material don't feel they're simply jumping through hoops for their certification, several of the sessions include a fifteen-minute period for those who have done this extra work to present what they've learned. Depending on the number of Extra Mile students in your group, this will require some judgment calls on your part to keep to the time frame.

Not every session includes an Extra Mile presentation. When the Extra Mile work has been personal and reflective, sharing of these assignments has not been included so that students might feel freer in their expression. The presentations are suggested, however, when the homework has included extra research on a topic related to the subject of the particular session.

Please make private notes about these presentations that briefly answer the following questions:

- **Who made a presentation?**
- **Did the presentation reflect that the assignment had been done?**
- Any other notes you believe would be helpful in judging whether **the student has done the appropriate level of work for the extra recognition they are to receive.**

While the Extra Mile work is required for certification and CEUs, others are welcome to do these exercises if they wish. If they do, they should be encouraged to share their findings along with the others. Be sure to keep the same set of notes for these students as well, just in case they decide at some point during the course to go for the certificate or CEUs.

At the conclusion of the course, these private notes should be submitted to the Massachusetts Bible Society to help with student evaluation. Most of the Extra Mile assignments include some written work. Students should keep these in a folder and submit them to the Massachusetts Bible Society at the conclusion of the course.

If you have a group (or a particular session) with no Extra Mile students, give the extra time to one or more of the other session activities.

First and Last Sessions

The first session of each course includes elements to help the group begin to get to know each other and lay the groundwork for future class sessions. There is some kind of icebreaker, a review of the nature and scope of the series, and guidelines for establishing a Bible study covenant.

It is always helpful if students can get books ahead of the first class and begin reading, but there are many reasons why that might not be possible. The exercises in the first session always assume that students have not read the first session of the Student Text. These exercises will have students actively using their student books more than in later sessions, where they will use the Bible more than their Student Texts.

The last session of each course is also a bit different. There is time in these lesson plans for both oral and written evaluation, celebration of the students' achievement, presentation of certificates, and housekeeping issues. The exercises in these sessions often reflect back on the course as a whole.

There are two kinds of certificates for each course. Informal students get a Certificate of Participation. These are available at exploringthebible.org/forms for you to download, fill out, and give directly to your students.

Extra Mile students get a Certificate of Completion. These must be requested from the Massachusetts Bible Society. You are prompted to send the information to us at the conclusion of session four so that there will be time to process these certificates and get them to you for the final session.

Lesson Plan

SON OF MAN 1

Objectives
- To help the group begin to know one another and to work through the first session of the Student Text.
- To familiarize students with some aspects of life in first-century Nazareth.
- To examine two important Gospel narratives about the life of Jesus.

Materials Needed
- Nametags and markers
- Newsprint and stand, whiteboard, or other means of posting information before students, and the appropriate markers
- Several study Bibles in different translations and with different perspectives
- Student Text for each student (unless procured ahead of time)
- Simple refreshments if appropriate to the setting are always a nice touch at every session, but especially at the first and last.

Handouts
- Life in Nazareth Quiz (p. 53)
- Class Contact Information Form (p. 51) You will need just one copy to circulate.

Leader Preparation
- Read the introductory and Session 1 materials in the Student Text.
- Read the introductory materials in this Leader's Guide.
- Review the Life in Nazareth Quiz on p. 67 and the answer key at the end of the Icebreaker session.
- Review the Session 1 outline in the Leader's Guide in detail.
- Find and prepare needed materials.

Gathering

The initial class announcement should invite students to come ten to fifteen minutes before the actual start of the ninety-minute session. During this time, each student should receive a nametag and their Student Text (if not procured ahead of time). It is always a nice gesture to have simple refreshments available. Make sure students add their contact information to the Class Contact list, and be sure to determine which, if any, of the students will be doing the class for certification or CEUs.

Make sure students are aware of the following regarding their contact information:

- During the course the information will be used by the group leader to contact students about course matters.
- Unless otherwise indicated, contact information will be shared with the Massachusetts Bible Society at the end of the course.
- The Massachusetts Bible Society will not share that information with any third party.
- Students will then receive one e-mail from the Massachusetts Bible Society to determine how much and what kind of contact a student would like to receive going forward. These options might include:
  - *Being a part of the regular Massachusetts Bible Society mailing list*
  - *Receiving information related to future Exploring the Bible courses, conferences, or activities*
  - *Receiving all event notifications from the Massachusetts Bible Society*

Session 1 Activities

Icebreaker: Life in Nazareth (15 Min)

As students arrive, give each one a copy of the Life In Nazareth Quiz on p. 67 of this guide. Pages 13-18 of the Student Text describe life in first-century Nazareth, and all the answers can be found there. Once everyone has a copy of the quiz, read the instructions from the handout to the group.

When time is up, gather the group together for the Group Covenant reflection. Latecomers may not have finished, but they will read the section (and therefore discover the answers) as part of their homework.

Welcome and Group Covenant Reflection (10 Min)

Objective: To make sure group members are familiar with Exploring the Bible and have some basic ground rules for interaction.

Welcome students to Course 3 of <u>Exploring the Bible: The Dickinson Series</u>. Introduce yourself if necessary. If there are students who have not done any other courses in the series, refer them to the introduction to the series on p. iii of their Student Text for information about the program.

Ask students to turn to p. 2 of the Student Text, where there is a bulleted list of facts about Jesus. Explain that, although scholars disagree about a lot of things, this list represents points on which virtually all scholars agree. Then, going around the room, invite a different person to read each bullet point aloud.

Notes

Session 1 Activities

Notes

When they have finished, explain that your group, like biblical scholars, will have a variety of opinions during class sessions. However, your group also can agree on a basic set of ground rules for your time together.

Groups that have followed the typical progression of this series will have already developed their own details of a group covenant in Courses 1 and 2. Just review the basics of that covenant here, referencing the Covenant for Bible Study in Appendix 7 in the Student Text.

A Covenant For Bible Study

We covenant together to deal with our differences in a spirit of mutual respect and to refrain from actions that may harm the emotional and physical well-being of others.

The following principles will guide our actions:

- We will treat others whose views may differ from our own with the same courtesy we would want to receive ourselves.
- We will listen with a sincere desire to understand the point of view being expressed by another person, especially if it is different from our own.
- We will respect each other's ideas, feelings, and experiences.
- We will refrain from blaming or judging in our attitude and behavior towards others.

Session 1 Activities

- We will communicate directly with any person with whom we may disagree in a respectful and constructive way.
- We will seek feedback to ensure that we have truly understood each other in our communications.

Additional agreements for our particular group:

Notes

Session 1 Activities

Notes

Bible Activity: Betrayed (30 Min)

Objectives: To remind students that the same stories are often told in different ways in the Bible. To encourage them to think about how they can explore and explain these differences.

Part I (15 Min)

- Remind students that the Bible contains four separate accounts of Jesus' life. Explain that in this exercise they will look at the similarities and the differences in the way these four Gospel writers tell the story of Jesus' betrayal and arrest.

- Divide the class in half.

- Ask one group to read and compare Matthew 26:36–57 and Luke 22:39–54.

- Ask the other group to read and compare Mark 14:32–53 and John 18:1–14.

- Ask both groups to make notes about the similarities and differences in their respective stories and to appoint someone to report back on the group's behalf.

Part II (15 Min)

- Ask each group to report on their findings.

- Explain that when they read the full text of Session 1 for homework, they will see some of the tools scholars use to find out why the accounts have those similarities and differences.

Session 1 Activities

- Remind students that their study Bibles will often have:
  - *Notes about why the account is different from the same basic story in another Gospel.*
  - *Cross references to other Gospels where the same story is told.*
  - *References to other parts of the Bible that might be related to the text (e.g., an Old Testament prophecy).*
  - *Information about fragmented texts, uncertain translations, or other textual issues that might be present in the original manuscript.*
- Discuss the following questions:
  - *Did anything surprise you in this exercise?*
  - *Do you think the differences you found are meant to be merged into one account or do you think they just represent different views of how the events took place?*

Life Connection Activity: Temptations (30 Min)

Objectives: *To make students familiar with a well-known Bible story. To encourage reflection on the nature of temptation.*

Part 1 (15 Min)

- Explain that three of the four Gospels have a story about Jesus being tempted in the wilderness and that you will look at the version in Luke for this exercise.

Notes

Session 1 Activities

Notes

- Ask a volunteer to read Luke 4:1–13 aloud to the group. Before the volunteer begins, ask the group to listen for one word or phrase that strikes them for whatever reason, and to jot that word or phrase down.

- When the person has finished reading, ask each person to share that one word or phrase that struck them. They should not comment beyond that about why or anything. Just have them say the word or phrase.

- Ask a different volunteer to read the same passage again. This time ask people to listen for the different kinds of temptations Jesus faces.

- Have people share the temptations they identified. Again this is quick: They are not to analyze them—just name them as best they can. You don't need to distill or group the responses. People might see several kinds of temptation in each promise offered by the devil in the passage. That's fine.

Part II *(15 Min)*

- Divide the class into small groups of two to three.

- Ask a third volunteer to read the same passage to the group.

- Ask each group to reflect on the following questions:
  - *Do you think the temptations Jesus faced were unique to Jesus or more universal to human beings?*
  - *How did Jesus overcome his temptations?*
  - *Do you think some people are just better equipped to deal with temptation than others?*

Session 1 Activities

- *How can we resist temptations more effectively?*

REVIEW the homework for the next session on page 27 of the Student Text, making sure students understand the difference between the homework for informal and Extra Mile students. (5 Min):

Homework (All Students)

- ☐ Read all of Sessions 1 and 2 in your Student Text, including the Bible passages in the clear boxes. Think about the reflection questions you find along the way.

- ☐ Begin reading the Gospel of Luke with a goal of finishing the entire gospel by the end of Session 3. There are twenty-four chapters in Luke so you'll need to do approximately twelve chapters per week to finish by Session 3. If you want to keep going, just jump into Acts. That's what you'll be reading in Sessions 4 through 6.

Extra Mile (CEU and Certificate Students)

- ☐ Read the section on p. 6 of the Student Text about the various types of criticism carefully. Research the "Q" source and write five hundred to seven hundred words reflecting on its importance to the gospels.

- ☐ Begin reading the gospels with the goal of finishing all four gospels by the end of Session 3.

Notes

Lesson Plan

SON OF DAVID

Objectives
- To examine the parable of the Good Samaritan and the Gospel accounts of the Last Supper.
- To allow students to become a part of these stories by reflecting on the events as a participant might have then or in a similar contemporary situation.

Materials Needed
- Nametags and markers
- Newsprint and stand, whiteboard, or other means of posting information before students, and the appropriate markers
- Several study Bibles in different translations and with different perspectives
- Sheet with Check-in questions
- Parking Lot list

Leader Preparation
- Read the Student Text for Session 2.
- Do the homework for this session listed at the end of Session 1, including the Extra Mile assignment.
- Research any questions that came out of Session 1 for which you promised a response.
- Write out Check-in questions on newsprint or whiteboard. (You can save doing this each week if you write on something that can be saved and brought back to each session.)
- Become familiar with the texts and activities for the Session 2 class meeting.
- Write out the questions for the Bible Activity and the Life Connection Activity and post them for easy reference.
- Find and prepare needed materials.

Session 2 Activities

Notes

Check-In (10 Min)

From this session on, begin each class meeting with a ten-minute check-in. Each session should include the following (brief) responses from each person:

- What is one thing that was new to me in this material?
- What is one question that this week's topic raises for me?

This is not the time to discuss what students have learned or to try to answer their questions. It's simply a way to note student observations and to spur the thinking of others.

Bible Activity: The Last Supper (45 Min)

Objectives: To help students become more familiar with the events surrounding the last meal of Jesus' life. To encourage reflection on the church practices that are based on this event.

Part I (20 Min)

- Divide the class in half.
- Ask one group to open their Bibles to Luke 22:7–34.
- Ask the other group to open their Bibles to John 13:1–30.

Session 2 Activities

- Each group should answer the following questions about their passage:
  - *When and where does the meal take place?*
  - *Who was present?*
  - *What happens before the meal?*
  - *What happens at the meal?*
  - *What happens after the meal?*
  - *What is one thing you would like to know about this event that is not answered or described in the text?*
  - *If you could ask a question of one person who was there, who would you choose and what would you ask?*

Part II *(25 Min)*

- Bring the groups back together.
- Let the groups share their responses to the above questions with each other.
- Ask the entire class the following questions:
  - *What church practices come from these readings? (A: Holy Communion/Eucharist and footwashing)*
  - *Have you ever experienced footwashing as a church ritual? Did you find it meaningful?*
  - *What has been your experience with Communion/Eucharist?*
  - *Almost every church celebrates Communion/Eucharist in some fashion, but not nearly as many do footwashings. Why do you think that might be? [Note: There is no technical answer for this. It is just a question for reflection.]*

Notes

Session 2 Activities

Notes

Life Connection Activity: The Good Samaritan (30 Min)

Objectives: *To help students to become familiar with one of Jesus' most famous parables. To explore the resonance of this parable with contemporary life.*

Part I *(10 Min)*

- Ask students to turn in their Bibles to Luke 10:25–37, the Parable of the Good Samaritan.

- Explain that this parable appears only in the Gospel of Luke.

- Remind students that they have more information about the Samaritans, parables, and this parable in particular in the second chapter of their Student Text.

- Remind students that Jews and Samaritans hated each other for both ethnic and religious reasons.

- Students should have read the parable as part of their homework, however some may not have done so. Ask the following questions to be sure everyone gets the basics of the story:

  - *Why does Jesus tell this parable? What questions are asked of him?*
  - *In the parable a man is traveling from Jerusalem to Jericho. What happens to him?*
  - *Who is the first person to come by the scene? What does he do?*
  - *Who is the second person to come by the scene? What does he do?*
  - *Who is the third person to come by the scene? What does he do?*

Session 2 Activities

- *What is the answer to the question that began this parable?*
- *What does Jesus tell the questioner to do?*
- *How do you think Jewish listeners would have responded to a parable with a Samaritan hero?*

- Mention that some cities and states have laws called "Good Samaritan laws," which protect those who help someone in distress. There are also hospitals and other non-profit organizations with "Good Samaritan" in their names.

Part II *(20 Min)*

Divide the class into smaller groups of two to three people. Ask each group to discuss the following questions among themselves:

- What is Jesus trying to teach with this parable?
- What might be the reasons that someone today walks by a wounded person without helping?
- Have you ever either walked by or stopped to help someone in distress? What went through your mind? What happened?
- Jews hated Samaritans for both ethnic and religious reasons, yet Jesus made the hero of the parable a Samaritan and showed Jewish leaders being unhelpful. If you were telling this parable in a modern setting, what people would walk by and who would help?

Notes

Session 2 Activities

Notes

REVIEW the homework for the next session on page 58 of the Student Text. (5 Min)

Homework (All Students)

☐ Read Session 3 in the Student Text, along with each of the Bible readings listed.

☐ Think about the Reflection Questions.

☐ Complete your reading of the Gospel of Luke. To finish the story, read Acts 1:1–11, which was also written by Luke. You'll be reading the book of Acts for the next three sessions anyway, so that will put you eleven verses ahead!

Extra Mile (CEU and Certificate Students)

☐ After reading the Student Text for Session 3, you will have seen Jesus in three distinct ways. In five hundred to seven hundred words, write an essay describing how you see Jesus. Who is he to you? What questions do you still have about him? You will not be asked to share this with others.

Lesson Plan

SON OF GOD

Objectives

- To examine what Jesus claimed about himself in the "I Am" sayings in the Gospel of John and to delve into what he might have meant.
- To allow students to explore their own tendency to believe or doubt, using the experience of "doubting Thomas" and Jesus' resurrection.

Handouts

- I Am (p. 69-75)

Materials Needed

- Nametags and markers
- Newsprint and stand, whiteboard, or other means of posting information before students, and the appropriate markers
- Several study Bibles in different translations and with different perspectives
- Sheet with Check-in questions
- Parking Lot list

Leader Preparation

- Read the Student Text for Session 3.
- Do the homework for this session listed at the end of Session 2, including the Extra Mile assignment.
- Research any questions that came out of previous sessions for which you promised a response.
- Write out Check-in questions on newsprint or whiteboard. (You can save doing this each week if you write on something that can be saved and brought back to each session.)
- Become familiar with the texts and activities for the Session 3 class meeting.
- Write out the questions for the Bible Activity and the Life Connection Activity and post them for easy reference.
- Find and prepare needed materials.

Session 3 Activities

Check-In (10 Min)

Ask each student to respond to the following two questions about the Session 3 material they read for homework:

- What is one thing that was new to me in this material?
- What is one question that this week's topic raises for me?

This is not the time to discuss what students have learned or to try to answer their questions. It's simply a way to note student observations and to spur the thinking of others.

Bible Activity: I Am (45 Min)

Objectives: *To make students familiar with the famous "I Am" sayings of Jesus in the Gospel of John. To encourage students to think more intentionally about what each one might mean.*

Part I *(35 Min)*

Distribute the handout for this activity found on p. 55 of this guide. You should have one copy for each student.

Give the following instructions/information:

- Each Bible verse on the handout represents a saying of Jesus in the Gospel of John.
- These are seven statements that together are known as the "I Am" statements of Jesus.

Session 3 Activities

- Find each verse in your Bible and write the metaphor/symbol in the space on the handout. For example, if Jesus says, "I am the vine," you would write, "vine."
- Next look at the verses and paragraphs around the I Am statement and answer the following questions on the handout:
  - *Who is Jesus talking to?*
  - *Where are they?*
  - *Why are they there?*
  - *Is there a particular question or situation that Jesus is answering with his statement?*
  - *Does the statement stand alone or is it part of a larger story or teaching?*
  - *Does Jesus explain what he means by this statement or does he just let it stand?*

Allow students to work either alone or in groups, giving them thirty minutes to complete the handout.

Part II *(10 Min)*

As a class, discuss the following questions:

- Have you ever heard any of these sayings before? If so, do you remember where or in what context?
- Were any of these sayings new to you? Which ones?
- Were there any in particular that you liked better than others? Why?
- Did you find any of them confusing? Why?

Session 3 Activities

Life Connection Activity: Resurrection (30 Min)

Objectives: *To make sure students are familiar with the resurrection narrative. To allow students to explore their own tendencies toward faith and doubt.*

Part I (10 Min)

- Have several people take turns reading John 20:1–29 aloud so that the entire group hears the story.

- Remind students that there are differences in the way the different Gospels tell the resurrection story. Encourage them to read the differing accounts at home if they have not already done so (it was part of the homework).

- If your class members are familiar with the hymn "In the Garden," explain that the hymn is based on John's account.

- Explain that the phrase "doubting Thomas" comes from John 20:24–29.

Part II (20 Min)

Divide the class into small groups of two to three people.

Ask students to discuss the following in their groups:

- Is there a person in this story to whom you relate more than others? Who? Why?

- Do you tend to accept what others tell you or do you tend to want proof?

- Whichever your tendency is, do you remember a time when you did the opposite? Were you glad you did?

Session 3 Activities

- Why do you think Mary didn't recognize Jesus?
- There is a lot of talk about "believing" in these verses. What do you think people here are being asked to believe?
- In John 20:29 Jesus implies that those who believe without proof are somehow more blessed or happy. Do you think that's true? Why or why not? Does it depend on the belief?

REVIEW the homework for the next session on pages 98-99 of the Student Text. (5 Min)

Homework (All Students)

☐ Read the Student Text for Session 4, including the Bible passages mentioned, and think about the reflection questions.

☐ Begin reading the book of Acts with the goal of finishing the book by the end of Session 6. Acts has twenty-eight chapters, so you'll need to read nine to ten chapters per week to get through it.

☐ Turn to the map of ancient Asia Minor on p. 100 of this book. Using the maps in your study Bible, the Internet, or other resources, label the following items on the map:

Bodies of Water
- Adriatic Sea
- Aegean Sea
- Black Sea
- Mediterranean Sea

Islands
- Crete
- Cyprus
- Rhodes
- Samothrace

Notes

Session 3 Activities

Notes

Roman Provinces *(Note that these are a Roman designation from the first century and do not reflect current geography that might have the same name.)*

- Achaia
- Asia
- Bithynia and Pontus (shown together on the map)
- Cappadocia
- Cilicia
- Galatia
- Lycia
- Macedonia
- Pamphylia
- Syria
- Thrace

You will receive the solution and develop the map further during the next group session.

Extra Mile (CEU and Certificate Students)

☐ Select either the city of Corinth or the city of Ephesus and research what the city of your choice was like during the first century C.E. Write a five-hundred- to seven-hundred-word description of the city in the first century, and describe the role of your chosen city in the Bible.

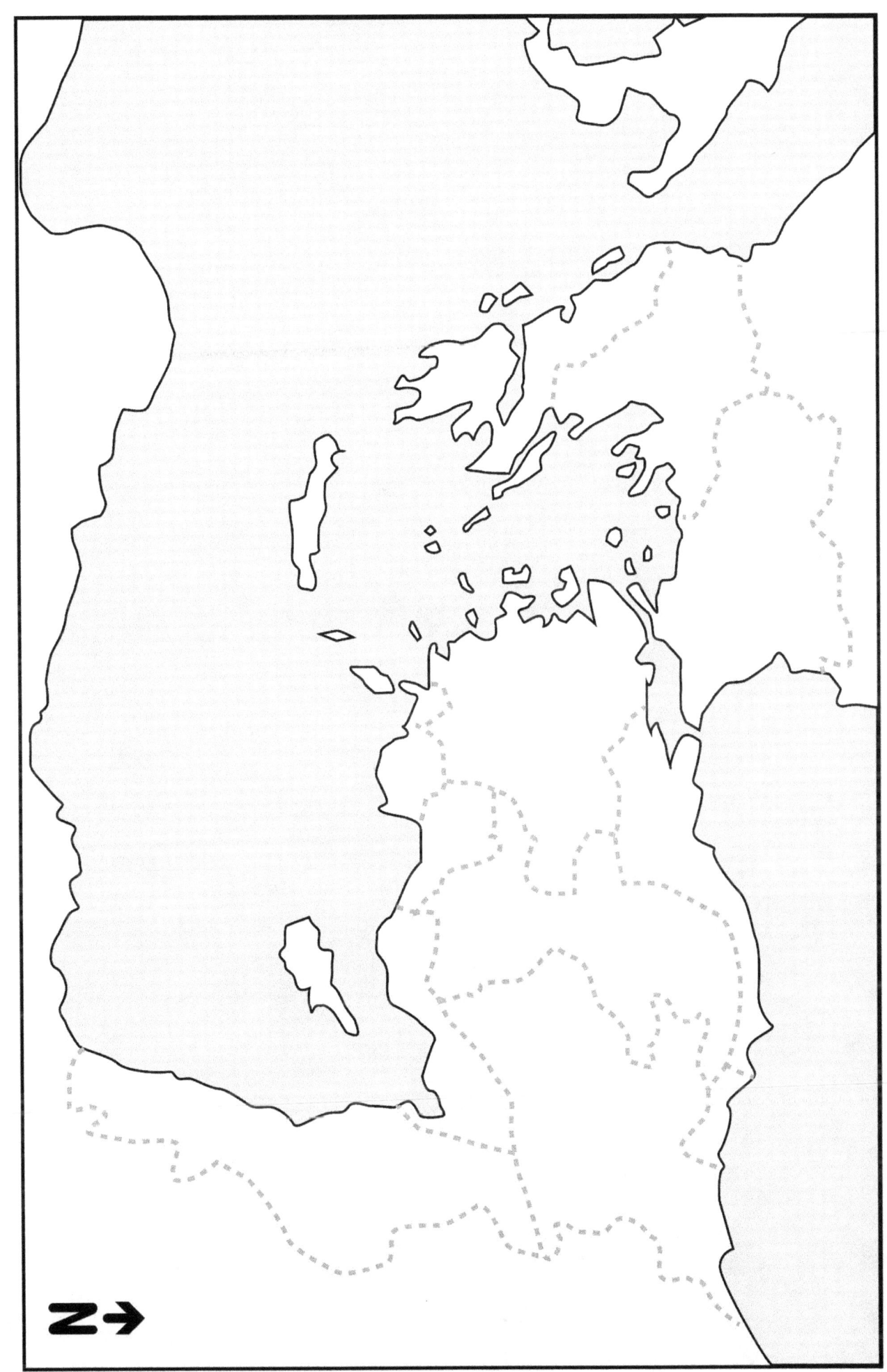

Lesson Plan

MAN OF LETTERS ④

Objectives
- To make students familiar with Asia Minor in the first century and the locations to which St. Paul traveled.
- To encourage a better understanding of the metaphor of the Body of Christ.

Handouts
- Connect the Dots Worksheet (p. 77)
- Connect the Dots City List (p. 79)
- Connect the Dots Solution (p. 81)

Materials Needed
- Newsprint and stand, whiteboard, or other means of posting information before students, and the appropriate markers
- Several study Bibles in different translations and with different perspectives
- Sheet with Check-in questions
- Parking Lot list
- A collection of materials to research maps. This might include:
  - *Study Bibles with maps in the back*
  - *Print copies of Bible atlases*
  - *Large maps of first-century Asia Minor. Often churches have these available for Sunday School use.*
  - *Internet access*
- Blank sheets of paper for the One Body exercise—two for each student
- Regular lead pencils with erasers for the One Body exercise
- Colored pencils and/or markers for the Connect the Dots exercise

Lesson Plan

Leader Preparation

- Read the Student Text for Session 4.
- Do the homework for this session listed at the end of Session 3, including the Extra Mile assignment.
- Research any questions that came out of previous sessions for which you promised a response.
- Write out Check-in questions on newsprint or whiteboard. (You can save doing this each week if you write on something that can be saved and brought back to each session.)
- Become familiar with the texts and activities for the Session 4 class meeting. Do the map activity so you have a better idea of where things are.
- Determine whether you want to do the map activity as a competition or not.
- Write out the questions for the Bible Activity and the Life Connection Activity and post them for easy reference.
- Determine whether you have any Extra Mile students and plan the time accordingly.
- Find and prepare needed materials.
- **If you have Extra Mile Students, contact the Massachusetts Bible Society to arrange for their Certificates of Completion. If you wait until the last minute, we may not be able to get them to you in time. The Certificates of Participation for informal students are available for you to download and fill out yourself from exploringthebible.org/forms.**

Session 4 Activities

Check-In (5 Min)

Ask each student to respond to the following two questions about the Session 4 material they read for homework:

- What is one thing that was new to me in this material?
- What is one question that this week's topic raises for me?

This is not the time to discuss what students have learned or to try to answer their questions. It's simply a way to note student observations and to spur the thinking of others.

Bible Activity: Connect the Dots (45 Min)

Objective: *To become familiar with the first-century map of Asia Minor and the locations visited by St. Paul.*

Part I (10 Min)

Ask everyone to turn to p. 100 in their Student Text to the map of Asia Minor they were asked to fill in for homework.

Give everyone a copy of the Connect the Dots Worksheet on p. 77 of this guide.

- Explain that the map has both the homework solutions and a new exercise that students will be doing now.

Session 4 Activities

Notes

- Explain that the purpose of the exercise is to become familiar with the first two missionary journeys of Paul as described in the book of Acts.

- Remind students that they are expected to read the entire book of Acts before the end of the course.

Divide the class into groups of three to four people, making sure each group has similar study helps and access to colored pencils, pens, or markers. You should also ensure that your star students are not all in the same group so that no one group has an extreme advantage.

Give each student a copy of the Connect the Dots City List on p. 79 of this guide.

Explain the following information and rules:

- Everyone in each group is to complete the map worksheet by identifying the locations on the city list.

- Every city location is already marked with a dot.

- All larger regions are already labeled (from their homework).

- Everyone will have thirty minutes to complete the entire exercise, which is in multiple parts.

Session 4 Activities

Ask everyone to look at the Connect the Dots City List you just distributed. Go through each section with the following instructions:

- Write the name of each location of Paul's first missionary journey near its dot. Look at maps in your study Bibles or any of the other study helps available. Work together.

- The locations are in the order Paul traveled, which will give you clues about where the next location might be.

- When you have identified all the places, draw a line in blue to show the route of Paul's first missionary journey.

- Do the same thing for Paul's second missionary journey, but this time draw the route in red.

- Find and label the Places of Note and mark them in green. Don't connect with a line. They are just places of interest.

- Find the cities with churches for which books of the Bible have been named and mark them with yellow. Don't connect with a line. Just circle or highlight them.

Make sure everyone understands what is expected.

Notes

Session 4 Activities

Notes

Part II *(35 Min)*

Give students a signal to start at the same time and watch the time carefully.

- Have extra copies of the worksheet available in case someone messes up and wants to start over.
- The team finishing first wins. (Prizes are optional.)
- If no one has finished at the end of thirty minutes, the winner is whichever group has done the most.
- When the competition is over, hand out the worksheet solution on p. 81 of this guide. This sheet has all the cities labeled but does not have the routes drawn.
- If students didn't finish or messed things up in their group, encourage them to try the activity at their own pace at home.
- Encourage students to keep their map for reference as they read the rest of the New Testament. Suggest the following additional activities:
  - *Add new locations as you read about them in the New Testament.*
  - *Figure out the modern-day names of these locations.*

Session 4 Activities

Extra Mile Presentation (5 Min)

Extra Mile students were asked to do research on either the city of Ephesus or the city of Corinth in the first century. Ask them to present their findings to the group during this time.

If you do not have any Extra Mile students, you can either add time to one of the other activities or use the time to deal with Parking Lot issues or other general questions or discussion.

Life Connection Activity: One Body (30 Min)

Objectives: To help students better understand St. Paul's metaphor of the Body of Christ and the differing gifts given to its members. To encourage students to think about an actual group to which they belong as an organic whole with complementary parts.

Part I (7 Min)

Make sure every person has two blank sheets of paper and something to write with.

Taking turns around the room, ask volunteers to read 1 Corinthians 12:12–31 aloud to the group.

Ask the following questions:

- Paul describes the church as if it were a human body with various limbs and organs, and Christ as the head. Do you think this metaphor is helpful?

Notes

Session 4 Activities

Notes

- What is Paul trying to say about the church by comparing it to a body? If a church or other group thought of themselves as a single body, do you think it would reduce or increase conflict? Would people recognize their roles or would everyone try to be the "important" parts?

Part II *(16 Min)*

Give the following instructions:

- Think of a group to which you belong. It might be your family, your workplace, your faith community, a club, even this class.

- Imagine that Paul is describing the functioning of that group in terms of his metaphor of a human body. Think about who does what in the group you just thought of and what body part each person might be. Be sure to include yourself. (Give a minute or so for silent reflection.)

- On one sheet of paper, list the body parts with the name of the person who best fills that role. Include the following guidelines/examples in your direction:

  - *For example, the person who typically runs the errands might be a leg, while the person who keeps up correspondence might be a hand. The person who talks the most might be the tongue. You might also include body organs. Who is the heart of the group? Who makes you step back and breathe (lungs)? And so on.*

  - *Think of as many parts as you can and consider who fills them, including the part that best describes your own role.*

INTRODUCING THE NEW TESTAMENT

Session 4 Activities

- *If more than one person does the same thing in the group you've chosen, it's okay to list them as the same part.*
- *Don't list a part if there is no one who does the function of that part.*

- Now, on the other sheet of paper, draw the body you have described, using only the body parts you listed. Yes, your body might have six tongues, two arms, and one foot. (**DO NOT put the names on the actual drawing.**)
- On a scale from 1 to 10, with 1 being "bedridden" and 10 being "running marathons," put the score for that body at the top of the page.

Part III *(7 Min)*

As people are finishing up, ask them to find one or two other people to share their drawing with. Share the kind of group you picked and, if you are comfortable, the body part you selected for yourself.

As you conclude, encourage everyone to think about ways to help the various "bodies" to which they belong to work together more smoothly.

Remind students that the end of 1 Corinthians 12 promised to show "a more excellent way" to work together. End by reading 1 Corinthians 13:1–13 to the group.

Notes

Notes

REVIEW the homework for the next session on page 131 of the Student Text. (5 Min)

Homework (All Students)

☐ Read the Student Text for Session 5, including the recommended Bible passages, and think about the reflection questions.

☐ Continue reading in the book of Acts, with the goal of finishing the book by the end of the course. To avoid last-minute overload you should be around chapter 20 by the time you show up to the Session 5 class.

Extra Mile (CEU and Certificate Students)

☐ Several books of the New Testament are attributed to John: the Gospel of John, the three letters of John, and the book of Revelation. Some believe these are all the same John and some believe they are different people. Research this question and in five hundred to seven hundred words summarize the arguments for both positions.

Lesson Plan

LEADERSHIP

Objectives

- To examine the nature of faith as represented in Hebrews 11.
- To help students recognize the influence of others on their own sense of faith, morality, and virtue.

Materials Needed

- Newsprint and stand, whiteboard, or other means of posting information before students, and the appropriate markers
- Several study Bibles in different translations and with different perspectives
- Sheet with Check-in questions
- Parking Lot list
- Sticky notes for the Life Connection Activity
- Artwork you may want to use to post the "cloud of witnesses" in the Life Connection Activity

Leader Preparation

- Read the Student Text for Session 5.
- Do the homework for this session listed at the end of Session 4, including the Extra Mile assignment.
- Research any questions that came out of previous sessions for which you promised a response.
- Write out Check-in questions on newsprint or whiteboard. (You can save doing this each week if you write on something that can be saved and brought back to each session.)
- Become familiar with the texts and activities for the Session 5 class meeting.
- Write out the questions for the Bible Activity and the Life Connection Activity and post them for easy reference.
- Determine whether you have any Extra Mile students and plan the time accordingly.
- Find and prepare needed materials.
- **Note: The two major exercises in this session are really one long exercise about Hebrews 11–12. They are divided in two to give you a general sense of where the shift should occur from examining the Bible passages to examining the connection to life and to keep the time relatively equal between those two emphases.**

Session 5 Activities

Notes

Check-In (10 Min)

Ask each student to respond to the following two questions about the Session 5 material they read for homework:

- What is one thing that was new to me in this material?
- What is one question that this week's topic raises for me?

This is not the time to discuss what students have learned or to try to answer their questions. It's simply a way to note student observations and to spur the thinking of others.

Extra Mile Presentation (15 Min)

Extra Mile students were asked to research the debate about the authorship of the various books of the Bible attributed to "John." If you have Extra Mile students, allow them to share their findings here.

If you do not have any Extra Mile students, you can either add time to one of the other activities or use the time to deal with Parking Lot issues or other general questions or discussion.

Session 5 Activities

Bible Activity: The Faith Chapter
(30 Min)

Objective: *To encourage students to think about the nature of faith as represented in Hebrews 11.*

Part 1 *(10 Min)*

Ask students to turn in their Bibles to Hebrews 11.

Explain that this chapter is known as "the faith chapter" of the Bible because of the first verse, as well as the "by faith" refrain that begins almost every paragraph of the chapter.

Lead a brief discussion of the first verse:
"Now faith is the assurance of things hoped for, the conviction of things not seen."

- What kind of "assurance" do you think faith brings?
- Are there other areas of life where you feel certain of things you can't see?
- How did you come to that certainty?
- (Note: The general point you're looking for is that in most areas of life we make leaps of faith and trust that what someone else tells us is true. For example, we trust what molecular biologists tell us about our DNA, even though we can't see it ourselves. We can't have every experience and every bit of knowledge ourselves. We live our lives with a basic level of trust in the information given us.)

Notes

Session 5 Activities

Notes

Explain that:

- The rest of Hebrews 11 is a list of the experiences of Israel's faith heroes.
- The assurance and conviction in verse 1 is illustrated in these examples.
- The examples are also meant to provide deeper assurance and conviction for the reader. We are asked to trust the experiences of the pillars of faith mentioned in the chapter and to feel assured ourselves.

Part II *(20 Min)*

Divide the class into three roughly equal groups.

Assign each group a different one of the following sections of the chapter:

- v. 4–16
- v. 17–29
- v. 30–38

Using the helps and cross-references in their study Bibles, each group should compile a list of every Scripture passage referenced in their set of verses.

- *For example, verse 4 tells the story of Abel making a more acceptable sacrifice to God than Cain does. That group would write down Genesis 4:3–5, which is where that story is first told.*

Students have seven minutes to write down every reference they can find and come up with a tally of the total.

- *This part of the exercise is more about learning to use the study helps than in getting the list exactly right or complete.*

Session 5 Activities

Bible Activity: The Faith Chapter
(30 Min)

Objective: To encourage students to think about the nature of faith as represented in Hebrews 11.

Part 1 (10 Min)

Ask students to turn in their Bibles to Hebrews 11.

Explain that this chapter is known as "the faith chapter" of the Bible because of the first verse, as well as the "by faith" refrain that begins almost every paragraph of the chapter.

Lead a brief discussion of the first verse: *"Now faith is the assurance of things hoped for, the conviction of things not seen."*

- What kind of "assurance" do you think faith brings?

- Are there other areas of life where you feel certain of things you can't see?

- How did you come to that certainty?

- (Note: The general point you're looking for is that in most areas of life we make leaps of faith and trust that what someone else tells us is true. For example, we trust what molecular biologists tell us about our DNA, even though we can't see it ourselves. We can't have every experience and every bit of knowledge ourselves. We live our lives with a basic level of trust in the information given us.)

Notes

LESSON PLAN 5: LEADERSHIP

Session 5 Activities

Notes

Explain that:

- The rest of Hebrews 11 is a list of the experiences of Israel's faith heroes.
- The assurance and conviction in verse 1 is illustrated in these examples.
- The examples are also meant to provide deeper assurance and conviction for the reader. We are asked to trust the experiences of the pillars of faith mentioned in the chapter and to feel assured ourselves.

Part II *(20 Min)*

Divide the class into three roughly equal groups.

Assign each group a different one of the following sections of the chapter:

- v. 4–16
- v. 17–29
- v. 30–38

Using the helps and cross-references in their study Bibles, each group should compile a list of every Scripture passage referenced in their set of verses.

- *For example, verse 4 tells the story of Abel making a more acceptable sacrifice to God than Cain does. That group would write down Genesis 4:3–5, which is where that story is first told.*

Students have seven minutes to write down every reference they can find and come up with a tally of the total.

- *This part of the exercise is more about learning to use the study helps than in getting the list exactly right or complete.*

Session 5 Activities

After seven minutes, stop the groups and ask for a count of the number of passages they found, acknowledging that the listing might not be complete.

Add the number of passages up for a grand total for the chapter.

Ask the group to list names of public figures (current or past) who they think could be added to the list of faith heroes in Hebrews 11. Write them on the newsprint/whiteboard as they are named.

Now ask students to list character traits (apart from faith) that they think are needed to live such a life. Post those traits as well.

Have a volunteer read verses 39–40 to the group: "Yet all these, though they were commended for their faith, did not receive what was promised, since God had provided something better so that they would not, apart from us, be made perfect."

Move right along to the next exercise, which comes from Hebrews 12.

Notes

Session 5 Activities

Notes

Life Connection Activity: Cloud of Witnesses (30 Min)

Objective: To encourage students to think about and give tribute to those who have inspired them to become our best selves.

Part I (5 Min)

Give each student a little stack of sticky notes. (Note: These will be posted around the room with names representing the "cloud of witnesses" in Hebrews 12:1. Feel free to get artsy with the colors of the notes or the space where they will be posted.)

Ask a volunteer to read Hebrews 12:1–3 to the group.

Explain to the group that in the Bible the word "perfection" means "wholeness" or "completion." It doesn't mean never making a mistake or getting everything absolutely right.

Explain that the author of Hebrews sees that completion or perfection in the unity of all faithful people, something the writer believes was accomplished in the work of Jesus. The way this writer sees it, we cannot be "perfect" by ourselves.

Divide the class into smaller groups of two to three people.

Session 5 Activities

Part II *(25 Min)*

Give the following instruction to the small groups:

- It is not just public figures who inspire us. Take a couple minutes in silence and think of people in your own life who have given you an example of running the race with perseverance and endurance.

- As you think of those names, write each one on a separate sticky note.

- Put those sticky notes on the wall.

- Remain in quiet reflection until all in your small group have posted their names.

- Share with your group about the way one of the people you chose has inspired you. If time allows, you may share more than one, but be sure everyone has had the chance to share one before anyone shares more.

Notes

Session 5 Activities

Notes

REVIEW the homework for the next session on page 166 of the Student Text. (5 Min)

Homework (All Students)

- ☐ Read the Student Text for Session 6, including the Bible references mentioned.
- ☐ Think about the questions for reflection.
- ☐ Do a bit of online research and find one person (there are many) born after 1900 who has been called the Antichrist.
- ☐ Finish reading the book of Acts.

Extra Mile (CEU and Certificate Students)

- ☐ Do some research and find as many people as possible (of any era) who have been called the Antichrist.
- ☐ Reflect on the letters to the seven churches in Revelation 2–3. Considering the strengths and weaknesses of your own faith community or other group, write the letter you think God might send to your assembly.

Lesson Plan

EXPERIENCING **CHURCH**

Objectives

- To review what has been learned about the life, demeanor, and teachings of Jesus.
- To encourage students to reflect on their own lives in light of what they have learned.
- To celebrate the achievements of students who have completed the course.
- To evaluate the course.

Handouts

- Student Evaluations
- Certificates
  - Certificates of Participation for informal students are available for you to download and fill out at exploringthebible.org/forms. Certificates of Completion for Extra Mile students must be obtained from and signed by the Massachusetts Bible Society. You were instructed to request these in Session 4.

Materials Needed

- Nametags and markers
- Newsprint and stand, whiteboard, or other means of posting information before students, and the appropriate markers
- Several study Bibles in different translations and with different perspectives
- Sheet with Check-in questions
- Parking Lot list

Leader Preparation

- Read the Student Text for Session 6.
- Do the homework for this session listed at the end of Session 5, including the Extra Mile assignment.
- Research any questions that came out of previous sessions for which you promised a response.
- Write out Check-in questions on newsprint or whiteboard. (You can save doing this each week if you write on something that can be saved and brought back to each session.)

Lesson Plan

- Become familiar with the texts and activities for the Session 6 class meeting.

- Make sure you have enough space on your newsprint/whiteboard to make the three lists for the Christ and Antichrist exercise.

- Write and post the Wrap-up questions for easy reference.

- Find and prepare needed materials.

- Become familiar with the completion activities that follow this session to make sure your students get proper credit and can be made aware of future opportunities.

- Download, print, and fill out a Certificate of Participation for each of your informal students. Double check the spelling of their names. Certificates can be downloaded from exploringthebible.org/forms.

Session 6 Activities

Check-In (10 Min)

Ask each student to respond to the following two questions about the Session 6 material they read for homework:

- What is one thing that was new to me in this material?
- What is one question that this week's topic raises for me?

This is not the time to discuss what students have learned or to try to answer their questions. It's simply a way to note student observations and to spur the thinking of others.

Exercise: Christ and Antichrist (45 Min)

Objectives: *To encourage students to explore the qualities that make someone Christ-like, and to recognize their own strengths and weaknesses in striving toward that ideal.*

Part I (30 Min)

Note: You will be making three total lists, and the impact of the exercise is best when all three lists can be seen together at the end. If you are using newsprint, put each list up on the wall when it is complete. If you are using whiteboard, divide the space into three sections—don't erase a list when it is complete.

Notes

Session 6 Activities

Notes

List 1:

- Remind students that for homework, they were asked to find the names of people born after 1900 who someone (anyone) has identified as the Antichrist.

- Ask students to share those names and list them on newsprint or whiteboard. Use every name given. Don't let people start arguing about political figures or whether a name is appropriate. Just get the list.

List 2:

- Remind students that they have now read a lot of the New Testament and have gained a lot of information about Jesus.

- **Based on what they have read in the Bible and learned in the course**, ask students to share traits, attitudes, and actions that they believe are Christ-like.

- Encourage students to give reasons for the traits they add to the list. For example, if someone says "compassionate" and you ask them why they think compassion is Christ-like, they might answer "because he healed people." The point of this is to be sure the group doesn't lapse into just spouting off a list of common virtues or church doctrines. Try hard to get them to give evidence from the life of Jesus or other New Testament witnesses to back up the trait. Group members can help one another with this—there's no need to put an individual on the spot.

Session 6 Activities

- Try to condense each trait into one or two words, and write the list on the newsprint or whiteboard. You don't have to list the supporting evidence. Make the list as complete as possible and don't worry if different words overlap in meaning.

List 3:

- Remind students that:
  - *The word "antichrist" does not appear in the book of Revelation and only appears in John's letters.*
  - *John uses the word to refer to attitudes and actions that can and do exist in many people.*
  - *There is no single figure, past or present, that the Bible labels as the Antichrist.*
- Explain that the word means exactly what it looks like—someone who is the opposite of Jesus, who is in some way *anti*-Christ.
- Based on your list of Christ-like features, develop a list of opposite traits, attitudes, and actions. Again, try to condense each thing into a couple of words and don't worry about an overlap of meaning in similar words.

Part II *(10 Min)*

- Make sure each student has paper and a pen or pencil.
- Tell students they will make some personal lists, which will be for their eyes only.
- Ask students to reflect silently on List 2 (the list of Christ-like attributes) and compare those traits to their own lives.

Notes

Session 6 Activities

Notes

- Instruct each person to write down every Christ-like attribute they have acted on, even if it was only once and even if they failed to exhibit it at other times. So, for example, if they ever acted with compassion, they should write down compassion. If they were ever patient, even only one time, they should write down patience. And so forth.

- Now have students do the same with the anti-Christ list. Again, if they ever showed that trait or acted in that fashion, even once, it goes on the list.

Part III *(5 Min)*

Discuss the following questions:

- What, if anything, do you think qualifies someone for the label of "Antichrist"?

- Based on those qualifications, are there any people on List 1 that you would remove? Why?

Wrap-up *(10 Min)*

Remind students of the "Help! I Have Questions!" section on page 265 in their Student Text (Appendix 8) to resolve any questions that remain unanswered for them from the course material or to help with new questions that may arise from continued study.

This is a time to get oral feedback about the full course. The written evaluation is done in the Evaluation and Celebration below.

Session 6 Activities

- Appoint someone (maybe yourself) to take detailed notes about the responses to better inform your facilitator's evaluation.
- Ask the following questions:
  - *What were your expectations for this course and were those expectations met?*
  - *Did you enjoy the class activities? What was appealing about them? What wasn't appealing?*
  - *Do you understand the New Testament more (or less) now than when you started? How did this class contribute to this change?*
  - *Did this course make you more (or less) interested in delving more deeply into the New Testament?*
  - *Was there anything you learned about the New Testament that really surprised you?*
  - *Did you feel that the course was unbiased in its approach to the text?*
  - *Is there additional feedback you would like to provide to the Massachusetts Bible Society?*

Evaluation and Celebration
(10 Min)

- Collect any outstanding homework from Extra Mile students and remind them of the last homework assignment for this lesson on page 204 of the Student Text.
- Congratulate all students and hand out their certificates one by one. Recognize the hard work they have put into the course and sing their praises. Celebrate the accomplishment of your students!

Notes

Session 6 Activities

Notes

- Hand out the student evaluations and envelopes. Students should fill out the evaluations **during this time** and seal them in the envelope before turning them back in to you.

- Before letting students go, remind them that this is the third of three, six-week courses in Exploring the Bible: The Dickinson Series. They can continue to learn with courses from this series they may have skipped or with many other available Bible studies and materials.

Once the Final Session Is Complete

Mail the following back to the Massachusetts Bible Society:

- Student Evaluations

- Your Facilitator Evaluation

- Homework from your Extra Mile students

- Your notes about the performance of the Extra Mile students

- Your class contact list (See the note in the Gathering section of Session 1 on p. 2 for the assurances of how this list is and is not used.)

Session 6 Activities

Extra Mile (CEU and Certificate Students)

☐ In an essay of five hundred to seven hundred words, describe your experience of the New Testament in this course. What was new to you? What was familiar? Did you find your beliefs challenged? Supported? If you could take one lesson from this course back to your own faith community, what would it be? If you are not part of a faith community, would you recommend that others read the New Testament? Why or why not?

Notes

Session 6 Activities

Extra Mile (CEU and Certificate Students)

☐ In an essay of five hundred to seven hundred words, describe your experience of the New Testament in this course. What was new to you? What was familiar? Did you find your beliefs challenged? Supported? If you could take one lesson from this course back to your own faith community, what would it be? If you are not part of a faith community, would you recommend that others read the New Testament? Why or why not?

Notes

Please return this evaluation to:
Massachusetts Bible Society, 199 Herrick Rd.,
Newton Centre, MA 02459
or e-mail to dsadmin@massbible.org.

STUDENT EVALUATION

Course (circle one):   I   II   III

Why did you take this course? Were your expectations met?

Did you do this study with a group or on your own?   ☐ **Group**   ☐ **Alone**

Did you take this course for certification or CEUs?   ☐ Yes   ☐ No
If yes, please be sure that all of your written work is submitted to the Massachusetts Bible Society by either yourself or your group leader at the conclusion of the course.

Did your group have a mix of "Extra Mile" and informal students?   ☐ Yes   ☐ No

If "yes," did you find the mix helpful?   ☐ Yes   ☐ No

Why or why not?

STUDENT EVALUATION

Who was your group leader? _____

Scale: 1 - most negative, 10 - most positive

Please rate your leader on the following using a scale of 1-10.

- _____ Creating a welcoming and inclusive environment
- _____ Keeping the class sessions on track
- _____ Beginning and ending on time
- _____ Handling conflicting opinions with respect
- _____ Being prepared for class sessions

Scale: 1 - most negative, 10 - most positive

Please rate the physical setting for your group on the following using a scale of 1-10.

- _____ The space was free of distractions and interruptions
- _____ The space was physically comfortable and conductive to learning
- _____ The group could easily adjust to different configurations
- _____ It was easy to see instructional materials and group members
- _____ Restroom facilities were easily accessible
- _____ The space was accessible to those with disabilities

Do you have a particular faith tradition or spiritual orientation? If so, how would you name it?

_____

Did you feel that your opinions and perspective were respected in the following areas:

Course materials?	☐ Yes	☐ No
Class discussions?	☐ Yes	☐ No
By the group leader?	☐ Yes	☐ No

STUDENT EVALUATION

If you were an "informal student" (i.e., not a student seeking certification or CEUs), how much of the homework and reading did you complete? Please describe on a scale of 1-10, with 1 being virtually none and 10 being all of it.

_____

Did you do any of the Extra Mile assignments? ☐ Yes ☐ No

Scale: 1 - most negative, 10 - most positive

Please rate the quality of the homework assignments using a scale of 1-10.

_____ It was easy to understand the assignment

_____ The work could reasonably be completed between sessions

_____ I learned important things from doing the homework

_____ I did not feel pushed to come to a particular conclusion

Please answer the following questions:

Did you visit the Exploring the Bible Facebook page or follow us on Twitter @ExploreBible? Do you find these tools useful in staying connected to the Exploring the Bible community? Are there other ways you would prefer to be connected? If you would like to be on the Exploring the Bible e-mail list, please include your e-mail address in the space below.

Did this study answer any questions you had at the beginning? What were some of the most important questions that were answered for you?

STUDENT EVALUATION

Did anything disappoint you in this study? Was there something you expected that was not provided? Questions you really wanted answered that were not?

　

What new questions do you have upon completion that you did not have at the beginning? Do you find those new questions exciting or frustrating?

　

Did you learn anything of interest to you from this study? If you studied with a group, indicate how much of that came from the material provided and how much from the group discussion.

　

Have your impressions/beliefs/thoughts about the Bible changed as a result of this study? In what way?

STUDENT EVALUATION

Would you recommend this study to a friend?

How would you rate this study using a scale of 1-10, with 1 being not at all helpful and 10 being exceptionally helpful.

Other thoughts, comments, or suggestions?

Please return this evaluation to:
Massachusetts Bible Society, 199 Herrick Rd.,
Newton Centre, MA 02459
or e-mail to dsadmin@massbible.org.

Please return this evaluation to:
Massachusetts Bible Society, 199 Herrick Rd.,
Newton Centre, MA 02459
or e-mail to dsadmin@massbible.org.

FACILITATOR EVALUATION

Your Name: _____

Date the course began: _____

Date the course was completed: _____

Meeting location: _____

! **Course (circle one):**   I   II   III

Respond to the following questions about the demographics of your group:

How many were in the group at the beginning?

How many were typically in attendance at any given session?

What ages were represented in your group?

Did any drop out? If so, did they give a reason?

What was the gender representation in your group?

Describe the racial/ethnic representation in your group:

FACILITATOR EVALUATION

Did you have group members who self-identified as being of no particular faith tradition other than Christian?

[   ]

How many in your group were Extra Mile students?

[   ]

Please comment about your class dynamics:

Did you feel adequately prepared to lead this group? Is there anything this guide or more training could have supplied to make the experience easier?

[   ]

Scale: 1 - most negative, 10 - most positive

Please rate the Leader's Guide on the following using a scale of 1-10.

_____   The Leader's Guide was easy to understand and follow

_____   The class activities were appropriate to the session topic

_____   The class activities engaged the students in a positive way

_____   The class activities could be completed within the time allotted

_____   I always knew what to do in preparation for the next session

_____   I could fit preparation for sessions into my schedule easily

_____   The class flowed smoothly from beginning to end

_____   I was pleased with the overall quality of the Leader's Guide

FACILITATOR EVALUATION

Please respond to the following questions:

Did you encounter anything in class sessions that you felt unprepared to handle? If so, what?

To what extent did the students in your group know one another at the beginning of the course?

Did the group gain cohesion over the six sessions?

To what extent did the students do the homework and reading?

Did you personally enjoy facilitating this group? Why or why not? Would you do it again?

FACILITATOR EVALUATION

Other thoughts, comments, or suggestions?

Please return this evaluation to:
Massachusetts Bible Society, 199 Herrick Rd.,
Newton Centre, MA 02459
or e-mail to dsadmin@massbible.org.

Massachusetts Bible Society Statement on Scripture

The Massachusetts Bible Society is an ecumenical, Christian organization with a broad diversity of Scriptural approaches and interpretations among its members and supporters.

The following statement on the nature of Scripture represents the guiding principle for our selection of programming and resources, but agreement with it is neither a pre-requisite for membership nor a litmus test for grant recipients.

> The Bible was written by many authors, all inspired by God. It is neither a simple collection of books written by human authors, nor is it the literal words of God dictated to human scribes. It is a source of religious truth, presented in a diversity of styles, genres, and languages and is not meant to serve as fact in science, history, or social structure.
>
> The Bible has authority for communities of faith who take time to study and prayerfully interpret its message, but it is also important for anyone who wants more fully to understand culture, religious thought, and the world in which we live.
>
> Biblical texts have been interpreted in diverse ways from generation to generation and are always filtered through the lens of the reader's faith and life experiences. This breadth and plurality, however, are what keep the Bible alive through the ages and enhance its ongoing, transformative power.

A Covenant for Bible Study

We covenant together to deal with our differences in a spirit of mutual respect and to refrain from actions that may harm the emotional and physical well-being of others.

The following principles will guide our actions:

- **We will treat others whose views may differ from our own with the same courtesy we would want to receive ourselves.**
- **We will listen with a sincere desire to understand the point of view being expressed by another person, especially if it is different from our own.**
- **We will respect each other's ideas, feelings, and experiences.**
- **We will refrain from blaming or judging in our attitude and behavior towards others.**
- **We will communicate directly with any person with whom we may disagree in a respectful and constructive way.**
- **We will seek feedback to ensure that we have truly understood each other in our communications.**

Additional agreements for our particular group:

Class Contact Information

Your Name: _____

Date the course began: _____

Date the course was completed: _____

Meeting location: _____

Please provide your preferred phone number and e-mail address.

Name	Phone	E-mail

Session 1: Life in Nazareth Quiz

With one or two other people, find the answer to each of the following questions on the relevant pages in your Student Text. One of you should read the related paragraph(s) to the others in your group. Then each of you should share your personal response to the second part of each question.

1) Which one of Jesus' disciples shows the reputation of the town of Nazareth by saying, "Can anything good come out of Nazareth?" (Student Text, p. 14) What name do you use when you want to indicate a small town of no significance?

2) What was the population of Nazareth when Jesus was born? (Student Text, p. 14) What was the general size of the town where you were born?

3) What was the synagogue in Nazareth like? (Student Text, p. 14) Would you be comfortable if your own place of worship didn't have a formal building?

Session 1: **Life in Nazareth Quiz**

4) What did a typical first-century Nazareth home look like? (Student Text, p. 15) On a scale of 1–10, with 1 being the simplest and 10 being the grandest, what was the home like where you grew up?

5) What kind of work did a first-century carpenter do? (Student Text, p. 16) What was the primary occupation of your parents or guardians as you were growing up?

6) What indication do we have in the Bible that Jesus was born into a poor family? (Student Text, pp. 17-18) Did you have economic advantages growing up?

7) What kinds of foods did Jesus and his family eat? (Student Text, p. 17) What was a favorite dish in your family of origin?

Session 3: I Am

John 6:35

What is the metaphor?

Who is Jesus talking to?

Where are they?

Why are they there?

Is there a particular question or situation that Jesus is answering with his statement?

Does the statement stand alone or is it part of a larger story or teaching?

Does Jesus explain what he means by this statement or does he just let it stand?

Session 3: **I Am** — III

John 8:12

What is the metaphor?

Who is Jesus talking to?

Where are they?

Why are they there?

Is there a particular question or situation that Jesus is answering with his statement?

Does the statement stand alone or is it part of a larger story or teaching?

Does Jesus explain what he means by this statement or does he just let it stand?

Session 3: I Am

John 10:9

What is the metaphor?

Who is Jesus talking to?

Where are they?

Why are they there?

Is there a particular question or situation that Jesus is answering with his statement?

Does the statement stand alone or is it part of a larger story or teaching?

Does Jesus explain what he means by this statement or does he just let it stand?

Session 3: I Am

John 10:11

What is the metaphor?

Who is Jesus talking to?

Where are they?

Why are they there?

Is there a particular question or situation that Jesus is answering with his statement?

Does the statement stand alone or is it part of a larger story or teaching?

Does Jesus explain what he means by this statement or does he just let it stand?

Session 3: I Am

John 11:25-26

What is the metaphor?

Who is Jesus talking to?

Where are they?

Why are they there?

Is there a particular question or situation that Jesus is answering with his statement?

Does the statement stand alone or is it part of a larger story or teaching?

Does Jesus explain what he means by this statement or does he just let it stand?

Session 3: I Am

John 14:6

What is the metaphor?

Who is Jesus talking to?

Where are they?

Why are they there?

Is there a particular question or situation that Jesus is answering with his statement?

Does the statement stand alone or is it part of a larger story or teaching?

Does Jesus explain what he means by this statement or does he just let it stand?

Session 3: I Am

John 15:5

What is the metaphor?

Who is Jesus talking to?

Where are they?

Why are they there?

Is there a particular question or situation that Jesus is answering with his statement?

Does the statement stand alone or is it part of a larger story or teaching?

Does Jesus explain what he means by this statement or does he just let it stand?

Session 4: Connect the Dots Worksheet

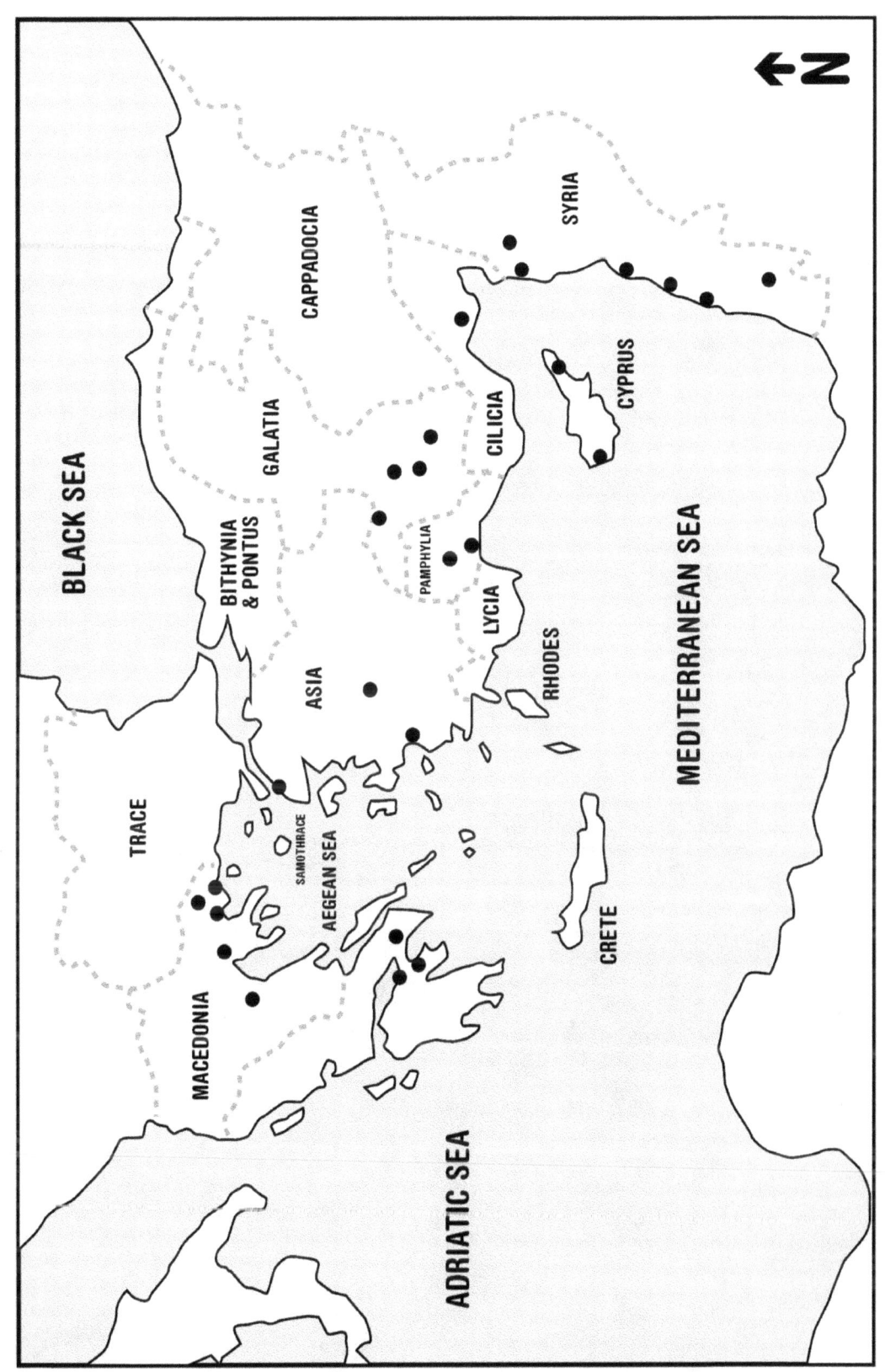

SESSION 4 HANDOUT: CONNECT THE DOTS WORKSHEET

Session 4: Connect the Dots City List

Paul's First Missionary Journey *(Label and connect with blue line)*

Going Out
- Antioch (Syrian)
- Seleucia by sea to…
- Salamas
- Paphos by sea to…
- Perga
- Antioch (Pisidian)
- Iconium
- Lystra
- Derbe

Coming Home
- Derbe
- Lystra
- Iconium
- Antioch (Pisidian)
- Perga
- Attalia by sea to…
- Antioch (Syrian)

Paul's Second Missionary Journey *(Label and connect with red line)*

Going Out
- Antioch (Syrian)
- Through Syria and Cilicia to…
- Derbe
- Lystra
- Through Galatia to border of Bithynia
- Troas by sea to…
- Samothrace by sea to…
- Neapolis
- Philippi
- Amphipolis
- Thessalonica
- Berea
- Coast near Berea, then by sea to…
- Athens
- Corinth

Coming Home
- Cenchrea by sea to…
- Ephesus by sea to…
- Caesarea
- Jerusalem
- Antioch

Other Places Of Note
(Label and circle or highlight in green)

- Tarsus (Paul's hometown)
- Thyatira (Lydia's hometown)
- Tyre (An important port mentioned in both Old and New Testaments)
- Sidon (An important port mentioned in both Old and New Testaments)

Locations of Churches Whose Names Became Books of the Bible
(Label and circle or highlight in yellow)

- Galatia (Galatians)
- Ephesus (Ephesians)
- Thessalonica (Thessalonians)
- Corinth (Corinthians)
- Philippi (Philippians)

Session 4: Asia Minor Map Solution

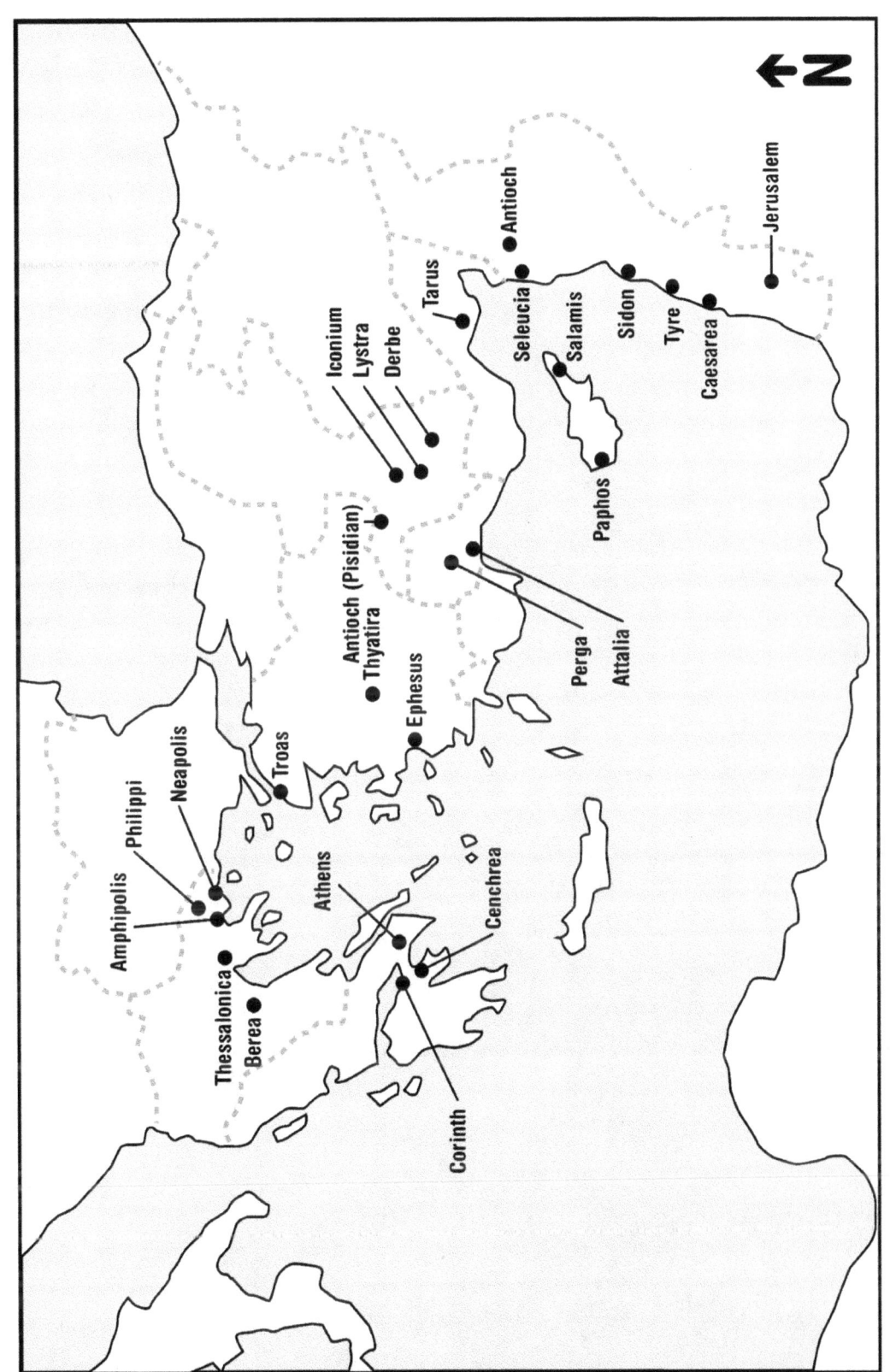

Sample Advertising Blurbs for Introducing the New Testament

Longer bulletin inserts, brochures, and/or posters can be supplied on request.

For Churches

"And she wrapped him in swaddling clothes and laid him in a manger." Jesus is the central figure of the New Testament. Course 3 in Exploring the Bible: The Dickinson Series, Introducing the New Testament, looks at Jesus in three distinct ways: A man like other men, a Jewish rabbi, and the Christ of Christian faith. Then it's on to the cantankerous Paul, the other New Testament authors, and the wild and baffling book called Revelation.

Learn what Nazareth was like in the first century, see what scholars know and don't know about Jesus as a historical figure, and decide for yourself whether Paul deserves either the stature or the censure that he so often receives from Christians. And who is the Antichrist anyway? Read, think, dialogue, and learn from this third segment in the popular series, Exploring the Bible.

[Add paragraph with the specifics of your course dates, times, locations, or other instructions particular to your church.]

For Secular or Mixed-Faith Groups

Who was Jesus really? What do we actually know about him and the time in which he lived? Where do the Christian beliefs and traditions about Jesus come from and how did Christian faith spread so far so quickly? Does the New Testament have anything to offer me if I'm not a Christian?

Course 3 in the popular Exploring the Bible: The Dickinson Series gives you the opportunity to learn about Jesus and Christian faith without pressure to conform to a certain theology or point of view. Read the New Testament texts and discuss the stories and issues they raise with a diverse group of people from a variety of faith traditions. Consider how famous parables like the Good Samaritan or the story of Jesus' temptations can resonate with everyone's life, no matter your faith or background. Won't you join us?

[Add paragraph with the specifics of your course dates, times, locations, or other instructions particular to your group.]

Glossary from Student Text

A.D.
Abbreviation for the Latin Anno Domini, meaning "in the year of the Lord." A system of notating time, generally used with B.C.

Antichrist
With a small "a" it is one who denies or opposes Christ. With a capital "A" it refers to a great antagonist expected to fill the world with wickedness but to be conquered forever by Christ at his second coming.

Apocalypse (adj. apocalyptic)
One of the Jewish and Christian writings of 200 B.C.E. to 150 C.E. marked by pseudonymity, symbolic imagery, and the expectation of an imminent cosmic cataclysm in which God destroys the ruling powers of evil and raises the righteous to life in a messianic kingdom.

Apocrypha
Books included in the Septuagint and Vulgate but excluded from the Jewish and Protestant canons of the Old Testament.

Ark
Something that affords protection and safety. Two different forms of this are prominent in the Bible. One is a boat—Noah's Ark—and the other is a sacred box—the Ark of the Covenant.

Babylonian Captivity (or Exile)
The period in Jewish history during which the Jews of the ancient Kingdom of Judah were captives in Babylon—conventionally 586–538 B.C.E. although some claim a date of 596 B.C.E.

B.C.
Abbreviation for "Before Christ." A system of notating time, generally used with A.D.

B.C.E.
Abbreviation for "Before the Christian Era" or "Before the Common Era." An academic and faith-neutral notation of time. Generally used with C.E.

Canon
An authoritative list of books accepted as Holy Scripture. The word is from the Latin meaning "rule" or "standard."

Catholic
With a small "c," the word means "universal." It is used this way in the Apostles' Creed. With a capital "C" the word denotes the Roman Catholic Church.

A B **C** D E F G H I J K L M N O P Q R S T U V W X Y Z

C.E.
Abbreviation for "Christian Era" or "Common Era." An academic and faith-neutral notation of time. Generally used with B.C.E.

Codex
A manuscript book especially of Scripture, classics, or ancient annals. A codex is bound like we are used to in a modern book instead of the more common scroll.

Codex Sinaiticus
A fourth-century, hand-written copy of the Greek Bible.

Concordance
An alphabetical index of all the words in a text or corpus of texts, showing every contextual occurrence of a word.

Conquest
The period of Jewish history described in the biblical book of Joshua. Many scholars believe the settlement of the Hebrews in Canaan took place over a much longer period of time and with less bloodshed than is depicted in Joshua. They would say that there was no actual "conquest" at all.

Covenant
A formal, solemn, and binding agreement.

Creationism
The doctrine or theory holding that matter, the various forms of life, and the world were created by God out of nothing in a way determined by a literal reading of Genesis.

Deuterocanonical
Of, relating to, or constituting the books of Scripture contained in the Septuagint but not in the Hebrew canon. Primarily Roman Catholic and Orthodox usage for the texts known to Jews and Protestants as the Apocrypha.

Diaspora
A scattered population originating from a single area. In this course the word refers specifically to Jews living outside of Israel.

Dispensationalism
A system of Christian belief, formalized in the nineteenth century, that divides human history into seven distinct ages or dispensations.

Evangelical
When used with a capital "E," this refers to those in Christian traditions that emphasize a high view of biblical authority, the need for personal relationship with God achieved through a conversion experience (being "born again"), and an emphasis on sharing the gospel that Jesus' death and resurrection save us from our sins. The tradition generally deemphasizes ritual and prioritizes personal experience.

Gilgamesh
A Sumerian king and hero of the Epic of Gilgamesh, which contains a story of a great flood during which a man is saved in a boat.

Hapax Legomenon (pl. Hapax Legomena)
A word or form of speech occurring only once in a document or body of work.

Hasmonean Dynasty
Those who ruled Judea in the late second century B.C.E. This represented a brief period of independence between the occupying forces of Greece and Rome and is described in the books of the Maccabees.

Hyksos
Of or relating to a Semitic dynasty that ruled Egypt from about the eighteenth to the sixteenth centuries B.C.E.

Inerrancy
Exemption from error. Infallibility.

Jerome
(ca. 347 C.E.–30 September 420 C.E.) A Roman Christian priest, confessor, theologian, and historian, who became a Doctor of the Church. Best known for his translation of the Bible into Latin (the Vulgate). Recognized by the Roman Catholic and Eastern Orthodox churches as a saint.

LXX
See Septuagint.

Mainline
Certain Protestant churches in the United States that comprised a majority of Americans from the colonial era until the early twentieth century. The group is contrasted with evangelical and fundamentalist groups. They include Congregationalists, Episcopalians, Methodists, northern Baptists, most Lutherans, and most Presbyterians, as well as some smaller denominations.

Marcion (of Sinope)
(ca. 85–160 C.E.) An early Christian bishop who believed the God of the Hebrew Scriptures to be inferior or subjugated to the God of the New Testament and developed his own canon of Scripture accordingly. He was excommunicated for his belief.

Masoretes
Groups of Jewish scribes working between the seventh and eleventh centuries C.E. They added vowel notations to the Hebrew Scriptures.

Mordecai Nathan (Rabbi)
Philosopher rabbi of the fifteenth century C.E. who wrote the first concordance to the Hebrew Bible and added numbered verse notations to the Hebrew Bible for the first time.

Orthodox
With a capital "O" referring to the Eastern Orthodox Church (and its various geographic subdivisions), the Oriental Orthodox churches (and their subdivisions), and any Western Rite Orthodox congregations allied with the above.

Ossuary
A depository, most commonly a box, for the bones (as opposed to the entire corpse) of the dead.

Pentateuch
The first five books of the Bible: Genesis, Exodus, Leviticus, Numbers, and Deuteronomy.

Pharisee
A member of a segment of Judaism of the inter-testamental period noted for strict observance of rites and ceremonies of the written law and for insistence on the validity of their own oral traditions concerning the law.

Protestant
Used here in the broadest sense of any Christian not of a Catholic or Orthodox church.

Pseudepigrapha
In biblical studies, the Pseudepigrapha are Jewish religious works written ca. 200 B.C.E.–200 C.E., which are not part of the canon of any established Jewish or Christian tradition.

Rapture
The term "rapture" is used in at least two senses in modern traditions of Christian theology: in pre-tribulationist views, in which a group of people will be "left behind," and as a synonym for the final resurrection generally.

Robert Stephanus
Protestant book printer living in France in the sixteenth century who divided the chapters of the New Testament into the verses we have today.

Septuagint or LXX
An ancient Greek translation of the Hebrew Scriptures. Translation began in the third century B.C.E. with the Pentateuch and continued for several centuries.

Stephen Langton
Theology professor in Paris and archbishop of Canterbury in the thirteenth century who first added chapter divisions to the Bible.

Supersessionism
The idea that God's covenant with Christians supersedes and therefore displaces God's covenant with Israel.

Synoptic Gospels
From the Greek meaning to "see alike," the Synoptics are Matthew, Mark, and Luke.

Testament
With a capital "T" it means either of the two main divisions of the Bible: the Old Testament or the New Testament. With a small "t" the word simply means a covenant or agreement that is formalized in writing and witnessed.

Tetragrammaton
The four consonants in Exodus 3:14 (YHWH) that comprise God's name.

Vulgate
The late fourth-century Latin translation of the Bible done by St. Jerome.

THE **IDEAL DVD PAIRING** FOR

Exploring the Bible

Produced by the Massachusetts Bible Society and The Walker Group, LLC, the 28-minute video **One Book, Many Voices** will let you hear directly from scholars, clergy, and just regular folks helping you to reflect on these questions:

- **How do YOU understand the Bible?**
- **Can we trust what is in the Bible?**
- **Is there a right or wrong way to read it?**

To view the trailer and/or order a physical copy of the DVD, go to **massbible.org/DVD**.
To buy or rent a streaming download, either search amazon.com for "One Book, Many Voices" or scan the QR code with your smart phone.

Help More People Explore the Bible

Your gift of $25, $50, $100, or more supports *Exploring the Bible* scholarships, study Bibles for those in need, and helps keep our training events at a reasonable cost.

$ _____ ○ One-Time Donation   ○ Recurring

Name

Address

Phone   Email

                                         ○ Check Enclosed
Credit Card Number

                                         Mail this completed form to:
                                         Massachusetts Bible Society
Expiration Date   Security Code   199 Herrick Rd., Newton Centre, MA 02459

You can also donate by calling 617.969.9404,
by e-mail at dsadmin@massbible.org, or online at exploringthebible.org.

www.ingramcontent.com/pod-product-compliance
Lightning Source LLC
Chambersburg PA
CBHW080444110426

42743CB00016B/3267